D0900071

SHAKESPEARE'S
WORDPLAY

Shakespeare's Wordplay

M. M. MAHOOD

METHUEN & CO. LTD.
11, NEW FETTER LANE, LONDON E.C.4.

FIRST PUBLISHED IN 1957
REPRINTED IN 1965

FIRST PUBLISHED AS A UNIVERSITY PAPERBACK
IN 1968

SBN 416 29560 6

PRINTED IN GREAT BRITAIN BY
FLETCHER AND SON LTD, NORWICH

DISTRIBUTED IN THE USA BY
BARNES & NOBLE INC

CONTENTS

PREFACE

In this investigation of Shakespeare's wordplay, I have sometimes found myself straying into fields of study which were new to me; but I have had the good fortune to meet with experts who, whatever they might think of the purpose of my journey, have generously given time and trouble to putting me on the right track. Dr Michael Argyle has kindly helped me to find out what the psychologists have to say about puns. I have been privileged to draw upon Dr E. J. Dobson's knowledge of Elizabethan pronunciation in order to verify the handful of homonymic puns which are discussed here. In disentangling the meanings of semantic wordplay, my prime debt has been to the printed labours of Alexander Schmidt, Dr C. T. Onions, the compilers of the *New English Dictionary*, and to Dr J. Dover Wilson in the notes and glossaries to his New Cambridge edition. Mr Redmond O'Hanlon, who has in preparation a Dictionary of Shakespearean Puns, has readily and patiently answered all my queries. I am especially grateful to Mr John Crow for many helpful suggestions and comments made when this study was in the draft stage. Part of Chapter One has already appeared in *Essays in Criticism*, and is reprinted here by kind permission of the Editor, Mr F. W. Bateson.

M. M. Mahood

University College,
Ibadan

I

THE FATAL CLEOPATRA

Wordplay was a game the Elizabethans played seriously. Shakespeare's first audience would have found a noble climax in the conclusion of Mark Antony's lament over Caesar:

> O World! thou wast the Forrest to this *Hart*,
> And this indeed, O World, the *Hart* of thee,

just as they would have relished the earnest pun of Hamlet's reproach to Gertrude:

> Could you on this faire Mountaine leaue to feed,
> And batten on this *Moore?*[1]

To Elizabethan ways of thinking, there was plenty of authority for these eloquent devices. It was to be found in Scripture (*Tu es Petrus . . .*) and in the whole line of rhetoricians, from Aristotle and Quintilian, through the neo-classical textbooks that Shakespeare read perforce at school, to the English writers such as Puttenham whom he read later for his own advantage as a poet. Dr Johnson's protest that a quibble was to Shakespeare 'the fatal Cleopatra for which he lost the world and was content to lose it' itself contains a pregnant quibble. Cleopatra was fatal in being both the death and destiny of Antony; and however Shakespeare's puns may have endangered his reputation with the Augustans, he was destined by his age and education to play with words.

Puns were repugnant to Johnson because a linguistic revo-

---

[1] Unless otherwise stated, quotations from Shakespeare's plays are from Methuen's 1910 facsimile of the First Folio and quotations from the poems are from the New Variorum Edition, edited by Hyder Rollins (*The Poems*, 1938; *The Sonnets*, 1944). I have not reproduced the italics from these texts, but have italicised the words played upon. Line and scene references are to W. Craig's one-volume Oxford edition.

9

lution as far-reaching in its effects as the Great Rebellion separated his verbal habits from Shakespeare's. Half a century after Shakespeare's death, Eachard put forward as a possible reform in education: 'Whether or no Punning, Quibling, and that which they call Joquing, and such other delicaces of Wit, highly admired in some Academick Exercises, might not be very conveniently omitted?'[1] The great aim of Eachard and his contemporaries was to make language perspicuous. It had accordingly to be freed of such prismatic devices as synonyms, metaphors and puns, Eachard sought to drive puns from the pulpit, Cowley's *Ode on Wit* celebrated their expulsion from poetry and the *Spectator* tried to blackball their admission to Augustan Society —to judge from the conversation of Swift and his friends, with small success.

Johnson's 'great contempt for that species of wit' is the aftermath of this Augustan cult of correctness and *le mot juste*. Yet Johnson's experience as a lexicographer quickened his response to the alternative meanings of words. The alertness which makes him spot (to give one example) the wordplay on *planta pedis* in 'some o' their *Plants* are ill rooted already' (*Antony and Cleopatra*, II.vii.1-2) will not allow more serious punning to pass unnoticed. 'Perhaps here is a poor jest intended between *mood* the *mind* and *moods* of musick' in Cleopatra's

> Giue me some Musicke: Musicke, moody foode of
> vs that trade in Loue,   (II.v.1-2)

and while he is 'loath to think that *Shakespeare* meant to play with the double of *match* for *nuptial*, and the *match* of a *gun*' he does nevertheless respond to the Citizen's pun in *King John*:

> for at this *match*,
> With swifter spleene then powder can enforce
> The mouth of passage shall we fling wide ope,
> And giue you entrance.   (II.i.447-450)

Although Johnson occasionally finds a quibble which is not allowed by modern editors—as in *Richard III*, III.i.128: 'You meane to beare me, not to beare with me', where he sees an improbable pun on *bear* the animal—he deserves our thanks

---

[1] *The Ground and Occasions of the Contempt of the Clergy* (1670), p. 33.

for his quick response to Shakespeare's wordplay instead of the blame he sometimes gets for failing to appreciate it. He shows far more perception in the matter than the nineteenth-century commentators. Shakespeare's Victorian editors, whose conflicting interpretations swell the *Variorum* edition, seldom saw[1] that all the meanings of a word might be admissible even though some must take precedence over others. The pun's credit was very low in the last century, in spite of Coleridge's repeated efforts to justify Shakespeare's puns on psychological grounds. Byron's attempts to revive a Shakespearean form of wordplay were little to the taste of the Victorians; and their own wordplay, if it surpassed the cracker-motto ingenuity of Hood, whose Fatal Cleopatra

> died, historians relate,
> Through having found a misplaced asp-irate,

had to hide in the nursery. Jabberwocky could be enjoyed only at seven and a half exactly.

Since then, Addison's worst fears have been realised; we have 'degenerated into a race of punsters'. Where the Augustans disapproved of Shakespeare's wordplay and the Victorians ignored it, we now acclaim it. A generation that relishes *Finnegans Wake* is more in danger of reading non-existent quibbles into Shakespeare's work than of missing his subtlest play of meaning. Shakespearean criticism today recognises wordplay as a major poetic device, comparable in its effectiveness with the use of recurrent or clustered images. The following chapters, although they attempt a fuller treatment of this aspect of Shakespeare's language than it has so far received,[2] are not and could not be

---

[1] Except unconsciously. See William Empson, *Seven Types of Ambiguity* (1947), pp. 81-2.

[2] Modern discussions of Shakespeare's wordplay which I have found particularly helpful are: E. E. Kellett, *Suggestions* (1923), pp. 57-78; J. D. Wilson's commentaries in his New Cambridge Edition, and Section IV of his Introduction to *Hamlet*; F. P. Wilson, *Shakespeare and the Diction of Common Life* (1941); Edward Armstrong, *Shakespeare's Imagination* (1946); William Empson, *Seven Types of Ambiguity* (second edition, 1947) and *The Structure of Complex Words* (1951); Kenneth Muir, 'The Uncomic Pun', *Cambridge Journal*, III (1950) and the same writer's New Arden editions of *Macbeth* and *King Lear*; Wolfgang Clemen, *The Development of Shakespeare's Imagery* (1951); and H. Kökeritz, *Shakespeare's Pronunciation* (1953).

an exhaustive and final discussion of the subject. The prosperity of a pun, like that of all poetic devices, lies in the ear of him that hears it; and however faithful to Shakespeare's intentions we try to remain by excluding meanings not current in his day, our acceptance or rejection of certain meanings, and the precedence we give one meaning over another, are bound to be matters of personal and subjective choice. With this in mind I have tried first, by a discussion of the functions of Shakespeare's wordplay, to quicken the reader's response to this aspect of his poetic art and so perhaps to add something to his enjoyment of Shakespeare. The ensuing studies of particular plays are more tentatively offered as a single reader's interpretation of the meaning of each play in the light of Shakespeare's delicate, ingenious and profound play of meanings.

1

The Art of Criticism, according to Bacon, has three branches: the exact correcting and publishing of authors; the explanation and illustration of authors; and 'a certain concise judgment or censure of the authors published'. Since Bacon's time, critics, although no longer concise in their judgments, have taken a smaller corner of the field of knowledge for their province; and his first function of criticism is now the preserve of scholarship. The mere critic would need a Baconian assurance to trespass into the field of Shakespearean textual study. But a detailed elucidation and appreciation of a Shakespearean play demands that we should be sure just what are the lines we are enjoying and trying to explain; so it may not be out of place here to indicate some of the ways in which a study of Shakespeare's puns can substantiate the findings of the textual scholar.

Textual scholars are now generally agreed that the so-called Bad Quartos which survive for seven (or counting *Pericles*, eight) of Shakespeare's plays are reported texts, representing either memorial reconstructions of the play for provincial performance by a reduced company, or the botched text produced by a single actor for unauthorised publication. In such a reconstruction we should expect the comic puns which got the laughs to survive, and the more subtle and subdued forms of

poetic wordplay to disappear; and this is just what happens in
such a play as *Romeo and Juliet*. Most of the quibbling between
the household servants and between Romeo and his friends is
preserved, but elsewhere there are losses—for example in the
marriage scene at Friar Lawrence's cell. In the Good Quarto
there occurs this exchange between the lovers:

> *Rom.* Ah Iuliet, if the *measure* of thy ioy
> Be heapt like mine, and that thy skill be more
> To blason it, then *sweeten* with thy breath
> This neighbour ayre and let *rich* musicke tongue
> Vnfold the imagind happines that both
> Recieue in either, by this *deare encounter.*
> *Iul.* *Conceit* more rich in matter then in words,
> Brags of his substance, not of ornament,
> They are but beggers that can count their worth,
> But my true loue is growne to such excesse,
> I cannot sum vp sum of halfe my wealth.   (II.vi.23-34)

The Warwick editor, J. E. Crofts, objects to this passage
because lovers at such a moment should not soberly discuss
music. He believes this to be one of the places where the Bad
Quarto has preserved 'what is evidently a distinct version, less
mature in style but probably authentic':

> *Rom.* My Iuliet welcome. As doo waking eyes
> (Cloasd in Nights mysts) attend the frolicke Day,
> So Romeo hath expected Iuliet,
> And thou art come.
> *Iul.* I am (if I be Day)
> Come to my Sunne: shine foorth and make me faire.
> *Rom.* All beauteous fairnes dwelleth in thine eyes.
> *Iul.* Romeo from thine all brightnes doth arise.

It is not beyond dispute that this is a more plausible version
than that of the Good Quarto and Folio; and it seems to me far
less Shakespearean. The received text is a beautiful example of
what Coleridge finely appraised as Shakespeare's 'never broken
chain of imagery, always vivid, and because unbroken, often
minute'. Here as elsewhere it remains unbroken because its
images are linked by unconscious wordplay. The idea of music
in Romeo's lines is produced by a shift in the meaning of
measure from 'portion or allowance (of corn)' to the sense of

13

tune or harmony, and by the ambiguity of *sweeten* which can apply to both taste and sound. Juliet, by her use of *conceit* to imply fantasy as well as thought, gently mocks the exaggeration of Romeo's words; but her own excitement reveals itself in a similar play of meaning, for she reverts to *measure* in the sense of portion and combines it with the fiscal meanings of *dear*, *rich*, and perhaps with the last element of *encounter*, to make a monetary conceit as hyperbolical as Romeo's musical one. The thoughts of both are quick and stirring, whereas the lovers in the Bad Quarto wearily mark time with a single laboured image until the Friar compels them to move on.

The Merry Wives of Windsor exists in a Bad Quarto version and its editor's task is complicated by the fact that the only other text, that of the Folio, is in the words of the New Cambridge editor 'strewn with verbal cruxes'. Most editors of the play have felt that the pirated version must be given a hearing; and the presence in its text of puns or vestiges of puns suggests that it is sometimes nearer to Shakespeare's own text than the Folio is. Falstaff, boasting to the disguised Ford that he enjoys the favours of Mistress Ford, is made to declare in the Quarto version: 'they say the cuckally knaue hath legions of *angels*, for the which his wife seemes to me well-*fauored*'. Shakespeare always found the quibble on angel coins irresistible, and here the actor-reporter (unless he wrote more than was originally set down for him) seems to have preserved a comic pun which is lost in the Folio's 'masses of money' (II.ii.289). He shows less skill earlier in the same scene, when Ford arrives at the Garter and is announced as Master Brook. 'Bid him come vp', says Falstaff, 'Such Brookes are alwaies welcome to me.' The remark has no point, but we can see from the Folio, where Brook is called Broom, what the point should have been: 'Call him in: such Broomes are welcome to mee, that ore'flowes such liquor' (158-160). Clearly the Quarto has preserved Ford's original alias even if it has bungled the pun, and all editors accordingly restore *Brook* in place of the Folio's *Broom*.

The most famous of these vestigial puns occurs in the first tavern scene of *Henry IV* part 1, where the title 'my old lad of the castle', given to Falstaff by the Prince, is a survival of the time when Falstaff was still called Sir John Oldcastle. There is here no question of a choice of texts, for soon after the play's first production the name was changed by Shakespeare, probably at the instigation of Oldcastle's descendants to whom he apologises in the epilogue of part 2. The Quarto of part 1 is a 'good' one, and the differences between it and the Folio are small; but it is interesting to see how, on one occasion, the wordplay supports the authority of the Quarto which is the basic text for modern editions. In this same first tavern scene Poins enters to the Prince and Falstaff with the greeting:

> Good morrow sweete Hal. What saies Monsieur remorse? what saies Sir Iohn Sacke, and Sugar Iacke? howe agrees the Diuell and thee about thy soule . . .

The Folio changes the punctuation of this passage to make 'Jack' an isolated apostrophe to Falstaff: 'What sayes Sir Iohn Sacke and Sugar: Iacke? How agrees the Diuell and thee about thy Soule . . .' (I.ii.125-7). But in following the Folio punctuation (with the modern mark of exclamation replacing the Elizabethan use of the interrogation mark) all subsequent editors have lost the wordplay of the Quarto. Poins is punning on *jack* in the sense of a tankard. Shakespeare had already used the quibble in *The Taming of the Shrew*, IV.i.51—'Be the Iackes faire within, the Gils faire without'—and Sir John Sack-and-Sugar Jack makes an apt soubriquet for Falstaff.

Occasionally the choice between divergent texts is made the more difficult by the possibility that the variants represent a subdued form of wordplay. This may be the case with Hamlet's first solitary outcry: 'Oh that this too too solid flesh would melt!' The Good Quarto, which is the basis of modern editions such as the New Cambridge, reads 'sallied flesh', and on evidence which includes Polonius's words later in the play— 'You laying these slight sallies on my sonne . . .'—Dr Wilson considers this a misprint for 'sullied'. 'Sallied' and 'sallies' may however be considered not as misprints but as alternative spellings.[1] Reynaldo is perhaps being told to besmirch Laertes'

[1] I am grateful for this to Mr J. Crow who cites as a parallel Dekker's *Patient Grissil*, I.i.12: 'Then sally not this morning with foule lookes', which may be a sally-sully portmanteau. See the full discussion by Fredson Bowers in *Shakespeare Survey* 9 (1956), pp. 44-8.

reputation by small sallies of wit or by brief sorties of detraction; while 'sallied flesh', although its dominant meaning must be 'sullied', may also contain the sub-meaning 'solid' which replaces 'sallied' in the Folio text. If so, what we have here is not a pun so much as a portmanteau word, for if Shakespeare delights to break one word into a spectrum of meanings he is equally ready at other times to fuse two or more words into a complex meaning. Sometimes the two words are already homonyms. In a phrase such as 'the great prerogatiue and *rite* of loue' (*All's Well*, II.iv.43) and some seven or eight similar phrases, *rite* means both 'rite' and 'right' together; and although Shakespeare frequently puns on *metal* and *mettle*, there are many places in the plays where the two words coalesce into one significance. Other portmanteau words are made from distinct elements. The Messenger in *Hamlet* likens Laertes' invasion of the palace to the ocean's 'inpittious haste' because he is both impetuous and pitiless to those who bar his way. Perhaps the richest example of this form of wordplay is to be found in Cleopatra's speech as she takes the asp from the basket:

> Come thou mortal wretch,
> With thy sharpe teeth this knot *intrinsicate*
> Of life at once vntye.   (V.ii.305-7)

Here, as I. A. Richards has shown, *intrinsicate* is not just 'intricate'. 'Shakespeare is bringing together half a dozen meanings from *intrinsic* and *intrinse*: "Familiar", "intimate", "secret", "private", "innermost", "essential", "that which constitutes the very nature and being of a thing"—all the medical and philosophic meanings of his time as well as "intricate" and "involved".'[1] The same kind of fusion takes place when Hamlet is made to telescope into a single word two of his insistent thoughts—that his flesh is polluted, and that it is a wearisome burden which he would be glad to shed. The editor's problem is to decide which meaning should dominate in a modernised version.

An ear for Shakespeare's wordplay can often help the editor when he is confronted by a crux in a unique text. For example,

[1] *The Philosophy of Rhetoric* (1936), pp. 64-5.

it justifies the emendation of this piece of dialogue between
Sir Toby and Sir Andrew in *Twelfth Night*:

> *An.* What is purquoy? Do, or not do? I would I had bestowed
> that time in the tongues, that I haue in fencing dancing, and
> beare-bayting: O had I but followed the Arts.
> *To.* Then hadst thou had an excellent head of haire.
> *An.* Why, would that haue mended my haire?
> *To.* Past question, for thou seest it will not coole my nature.
>
> (I.iii.98-107)

Theobald, seizing the antithesis between 'art' and 'nature',
brilliantly emended the last words to 'curl by nature'; and
he was proved right beyond the shadow of a doubt when
Rowe spotted the pun on *tongues* and *tongs*—that is, curling
tongs. The quibble here is an intentionally witty one. In other
instances the punning is unintentional, resulting from Shakespeare's verbal habit of association through consonance or
assonance, and recognition of this habit can often prevent us
from making needless emendations. A queer reading in the
text can be traced to the twists and turns of Shakespeare's
unconscious mind—although we have to remember that
copyists and compositors also have unconscious minds. Was
the vicar, or the printer of the parish magazine, responsible for
'The Armistice Day Service will be conducted by Cannon X'?
In *Pericles* III.iii.29, it was presumably the reporter, copyist or
compositor who produced 'unsisterd shall this heyre of mine
remayne' for the modern reading 'Unscissored shall this hair
of mine remain'.

An instance of associative wordplay which does really seem to
be Shakespeare's own occurs in the Duke's words in *Measure
for Measure*:

> We haue strict Statutes, and most biting Laws,
> (The needfull bits and curbes to headstrong *weedes*,)
> Which for this foureteene yeares, we haue let slip,
> Euen like an ore-growne Lyn in a Caue
> That goes not out to prey.   (I.iii.19-23)

Dr Wilson maintains that *weeds* is 'impossible' and accepts
Walker's *wills* in preference to Theobald's *steeds*. *Weeds*,
however, is not impossible, only irrational. Theobald's rational

steeds is good, because it echoes the image, used by Claudio in
the previous scene, of the body politic as a horse ridden by the
deputy. Shakespeare may have intended to write *steed*, but *weed*
is, I think, his word rather than the copyist's or compositor's,
because in its double meaning of 'tare' and 'dress' it fits
excellently into the thematic pattern of the play. The idea of
society as an unweeded garden had haunted Shakespeare since
he wrote *Richard II*; and the presence of a subdued plant-image
here is suggested by the just recognisable vestiges of one in
slip and in *o'ergrown*—'Oh fie, fie, 'tis an vnweeded Garden
That growes to Seed.' But the Jonson-like weeding-of-society
theme which gives the play its framework of the ruler spying
out his kingdom's vices is overborne by the tragic force of the
second theme, Angelo's discovery that his blood is not the
very snowbroth he believed it. 'Seeming, seeming': the notion
of disguise dominates the play, and Lucio's quotation of
cucullus non facit monachum unites the superficial and the deeper
themes. So in this passage the traditional idea of society as a
garden has blended with Shakespeare's concern over the way
official dress masks corruption, to displace the intended *steeds*
and substitute *weeds*. Perhaps it is bardolatry to keep Shakespeare's text so carelessly unblotted; but Theobald's emendation here seems to me an instance of Shakespeare Improved
rather than Shakespeare Restored.[1]

2

'Rightly to appreciate Shakespeare's puns', writes Sister
Miriam Joseph, 'one should regard them as examples of four
highly esteemed figures of Renaissance rhetoric—antanaclasis,
syllepsis, paronomasia and asteismus—which have their roots
in the logical distinction between the various meanings of a
word, and depend for their effect on the intellectual alertness
necessary to perceive the ambiguity.'[2] There is in fact a growing
tendency in modern criticism to approach Renaissance poetry
through its contemporary *Ars Poetica* to be found in the sixteenth-century books on rhetoric; but it is very doubtful that

---

[1] For another analysis of this passage see W. Empson: *Seven Types of Ambiguity*,
pp. 84-5.   [2] *Shakespeare's use of the Arts of Language* (N.Y. 1947), p. 165.

we could come by such means to a full understanding and appreciation of Shakespeare's wordplay. The nomenclature of the rhetoricians is not a helpful language for the twentieth-century reader who is trying to make explicit his pleasure in Shakespeare. Such a reader, who had been enthralled by

> To morrow and to morrow and to morrow
> Creepes in this petty pace from day to day
> To the last Syllable of Recorded time,

might try to appraise the lassitude conveyed in the falling rhythm of the first line, the way it passes into the metronome insistence of 'from day to day' to suggest Macbeth's mingled weariness with life and dread of its passing, and the skill with which these lines gather all the play's allusions to time into one massive statement. The comment of an Elizabethan reader —'E.K.' for example—would have been entirely different. 'Here', he might have said, 'we have an artificial *epanalepsis* in which our author somewhat affects the letter and brings us by way of a sweet *ploce* to a most cunning *catachresis*.' But every godfather can give a name. While the books of rhetoric can show us how the average Elizabethan was taught to embellish his Latin and English verses with tropes and figures, they tell us nothing of the poetic and dramatic function of these ornaments. Naming the parts does not show us what makes the gun go off. Moreover Shakespeare, although he must once have been an average Elizabethan schoolboy helped in his compositions by Quintilian and Susenbrotus, grew up into a most unaverage Elizabethan. His delights, like Antony's, were dolphin-like; they showed his back above the element they lived in. This extraordinariness of Shakespeare reveals itself best in the speed and ease with which he progressed from a rhetorical to a dramatic use of language, so that, while the personages in his earliest plays speak in Senecan *sententiae*, or Thoughts, the manner of speech of his characters soon changes to what Coleridge called 'I Thinking'. It would be possible to present this change as the counterpart of the contemporary movement in prose from the measured Ciceronian period to the broken, diffuse style which aimed to be the 'peinture de la pensée'; or of the movement in poetry away from the copious figures of words to a close logic based on Ramist rhetoric.[1] But Shakespeare is not a part of a literary trend, and in spite of our recently increased respect for his learning, Dryden's words about him remain substantially valid: he needed not the spectacle of books to read nature. His own observation and experience served to show him when and how people quibbled. When a pun is rhetorical in one of the mature plays, it is so because it is dramatically appropriate for the character to use rhetoric. There is an instance of this in the dissuasive oratory used by Westmoreland to the Archbishop of York, during the parley at Gaultree Forest:

> You, Lord Arch-bishop,
> Whose Sea is by a Ciuill Peace maintain'd,
>
> .   .   .
> Wherefore doe you so ill *translate* your selfe,
> Out of the Speech of Peace, that beares such grace,
> Into the harsh and boystrous Tongue of Warre?
>
> (*2 Henry IV*, IV.i.41-9)

Wordplay is also part of the persuasive rhetoric of the great set speech on Order in *Troilus and Cressida* where, like an Elizabethan preacher expounding his text, Ulysses copiously elaborates all the meanings of the word *degree*: degrees in mathematics, navigation and astronomy; degrees representing the ranks of society; degrees as rungs or steps ('the Ladder to all high designes'); degrees of academic attainment; degrees of descent ('the primogenitiue, and due of Byrth'); and finally the musical meaning of the word—'successive lines and spaces on the stave':

> Take but *Degree* away, vn-tune that string,
> And hearke what Discord followes.   (I.iii.109-10)

Except in a set speech like this, Shakespeare plays with verbal meanings, not because the rhetoricians approve of wordplay, but because his imagination as a poet works through puns, or

---

[1] See Morris Croll, 'The Baroque Style in Prose' (*Studies in Honor of Frederick Klaeber*, 1929); Rosamund Tuve, *Elizabethan and Metaphysical Imagery* (1947).

because his characters are placed in situations where it is natural for them to pun, or because puns help to clarify the particular view of life that he seeks to present in a particular play. Shakespeare quibbles as a poet, as a dramatist, and as a dramatic poet; and these divisions, though in part arbitrary, give us three means of approach to the functions of his wordplay.

In the 'headstrong weedes' of *Measure for Measure* we have already seen an example of the associative use of wordplay whereby the two or more meanings of a word link disparate thoughts or images. Often a vivid image owes its existence to such an unconscious pun, as in the dying words of King John. In a sixteenth-century sailing ship, the dead man's eyes (now the deadeyes) were the part of the tackle, consisting of paired wooden discs, which joined the shrouds to the channels. One kind of deadeye is called a heart.

> Oh Cozen, thou art come to *set mine eye*:
> The tackle of my heart, is crack'd and burnt,
> And all the shrowds wherewith my life should saile,
> Are turned to one thred, one little haire.
>
> (*King John*, V.vii.51-4)

This trick of Shakespeare's style is found as frequently in late as in early plays. An instance occurs at one of the most dramatic moments of *Antony and Cleopatra*, that of Antony's return from the sea-fight, defeated and, he thinks, deserted by Cleopatra:

> Heere I am Anthony,
> Yet cannot hold this visible shape (my *Knaue*)
> I made these warres for Egypt, and the *Queene*,
> Whose *heart* I thought I had, for she had mine:
> Which whil'st it was mine, had annext vntoo't
> A Million moe, now lost:) shee Eros has
> Packt Cards with Cæsars, and false plaid my Glory
> Vnto an Enemies *triumph*. (IV.xii.13-20)

Once again, the play upon the further meanings of *Knave*, *Queen* and *heart*, which produce the card-playing image, and the final pun on *triumph* in the sense of 'trump' may not be wholly unintentional, since sport and gaming are a leading *motif* of the play. But in a famous passage of *The Merchant of Venice* the wordplay appears to be entirely unconscious:

21

Por[*tia*]. Then must the Iew be mercifull.
Iew.　　On what compulsion must I? Tell me that.
Por.　　The quality of mercy is not *strain'd*
　　　　It droppeth as the gentle raine from heauen
　　　　Vpon the place beneath.　(IV.i.182-6)

Portia's *strained*, used to mean 'constrained', takes on the sense of 'filtered, squeezed through drop by drop' and so gives rise to a contrasting image of mercy poured lavishly as a blessing from the windows of heaven.

The clustering together in Shakespeare's poetry of certain images, which was first noticed by William Whiter in the eighteenth century, is sometimes made the more compact by wordplay. Perhaps the best example occurs in *Antony and Cleopatra*, IV.x.33-7, where the image-cluster of dogs, sweetmeats and flattery is clinched by *barked*—which incidentally lends weight to the emendation of *panelled*:

> 　　　　　　　　　　　The hearts
> That spaniel'd[1] me at heeles, to whom I gaue
> Their wishes, do dis-Candie, melt their sweets
> On blossoming Casar: And this Pine is *barkt*
> That ouer-top'd them all.

Elsewhere a double meaning acts as the quickly turned surfaces of an oarblade to move the poet's mind along the current of his thought from one image to another. There is a simple, rather leisurely example in the first scene of *Pericles*, where Pericles calls Antiochus's daughter a 'Faire Glasse of light' and 'glorious Casket' and then, with an unconscious play upon *viol-vial* shifts to the image:

> You are a faire *Violl*, and your sense, the stringes;
> Who finger'd to make man his lawfull musicke,
> Would draw Heauen downe[2] . . .　(I.i.81-3)

As a rule the connections are more rapid and intricate than this. At the beginning of Act IV of *Henry IV* part 1 Hotspur, who has just received news that his father cannot join forces with

---

[1] For Folio *pannelled*.

[2] Quoted from the Shakespeare Association facsimile of the Malone copy of the 1609 Quarto. *Vial* is a common seventeenth-century spelling for the musical instrument.

him, tries to hearten his followers by making light of their difficulties:

> Were it good, to set the exact wealth of all our states
> All at one *Cast*? To set so rich a *mayne*
> On the nice *hazard* of one doubtfull houre,
> It were not good: for therein should we reade
> The very *Bottome*, and the *Soule* of Hope,
> The very *List*, the very vtmost *Bound*
> Of all our fortunes.   (IV.i.45-52)

This is a good example of Shakespeare's most workmanlike verse, not heightened by striking metaphors or rhythms and yet animated by a nerve-like intricacy of meaning. *Cast* in the sense of 'a throw at dice' links with *main* in the sense of 'a stake at hazard', thus with the gambling sense of *hazard*, and so with *fortune*; there is, too, the suggestion of a final fling about *bound*. Or we can follow another strand of imagery in which *cast* in the sense of 'the cast of a net' begins a subsidiary image of seafaring, sustained in *main* (which has also the contextual meaning of the main power of an army), in *hazard* meaning a risk (such as a trading venture), in *bottom* meaning a ship or the seabed, in *list* meaning the heeling-over of a ship, and in *bound* in the sense of destination. Within this double series of images there are smaller connections: one between *bottom* as a ball of thread, *list* as selvedge and *bound* as margin; another between *read* and *list* in the sense of an inventory; and another between *sole* as 'footsole' and *bottom*, or between *sole* as 'single, unique' and *one* doubtful hour.

None of these submerged puns need escape our notice in a modernised text. But in *Macbeth*, modernisation obscures one of the best pieces of unconscious image-linking wordplay in Shakespeare. Where the modern editions have

> But here, upon this bank and shoal of time
> We'd jump the life to come,   (I.vii.6-7)

the Folio reads

> But heere, vpon this Banke and *Schoole* of time
> Wee'ld iumpe the life to come . . .

Dr Wilson declares *shoal* 'perhaps, after "a babbled o' green fields", Theobald's most brilliant elucidation. Accept it, and we see life as a "narrow bank in the ocean of eternity" (Johnson); reject it, and the image shrinks to the limits of a dusty classroom with Macbeth seated upon a "bank" or bench.' We may also accept both and thus experience one of those phantasmagoric impressions of enlarging and shrinking which are so much part of the total nightmare effect of *Macbeth*, and which we meet a little later in the same soliloquy in the babe, naked and newborn and yet striding the blast, or in the great apocalyptic horsemen which are also the cherubim, the infants of heaven. If a school-room image is undignified, there are many places in the play where Macbeth appears undignified, a small man dressed in clothes that were not made for him. Since *shoal* and *school* were not homophones in Elizabethan English,[1] we have here a portmanteau word rather than a pun, although the similarity of meaning between a *shoal* of fish and a *school* of porpoises may have helped the words to coalesce in Shakespeare's mind. Presumably he spelt 'shoal' *Schoole*, and in so doing admitted to his mind the meaning of 'school' which evokes the following image of 'we but teach Bloody Instructions'—just as the 'bench' meaning of *bank*, taken with *cases*, gives rise to the ideas of justice and judgment later in the speech. Theobald's spelling has, however, the merit of emphasising the meaning most relevant to the play as a whole. The shoal is not, I think, so much Johnson's sandbank in the sea of eternity as the momentous instant of choice in the flux of time; and the image adds itself to Duncan's flood of honours 'deep and broad', to the river of blood forded by Macbeth in Act III and to the Lethe of sleep and death, to make up the four infernal streams of the tragedy.

Sometimes a word, the various meanings of which offer the poet a range of images, itself remains unexpressed. George Herbert's poem beginning 'Love bade me welcome' is built upon the ordinary and the Eucharistic meanings of the word

[1] For this reason H. Kökeritz (*Shakespeare's Pronunciation*, 1953, p. 24 and p. 87) will not admit this as an instance of wordplay. But puns need not be homophones to succeed, as we can prove by switching on the wireless any Saturday evening. However, the wordplay in this instance is not so much auditory as orthographic and is quite involuntary. Some people produce orthographic puns whenever they write or type.

host which nowhere occurs in the poem. Such unspoken puns, whether conscious or unconscious, abound in Shakespeare's verse. When Queen Isabel says to the deposed Richard:

> thou most beauteous Inne,
> Why should hard-fauor'd Griefe be lodg'd in thee,
> When Triumph is become an Ale-house Guest,
> (*Richard II*, v.i.13-15)

the image becomes less of a conceit to us when we realise the wordplay upon the different meanings of *entertain*. The connection of ideas is fairly easy to grasp in *Twelfth Night* II.ii.56-8, where Sir Toby caps Sir Andrew's praise of the clown's song— 'A mellifluous voice'—with 'A contagious breath', since this is clearly a pun on *catch*. But Feste's 'As there is no true Cuckold but calamity, so beauties a flower' (I.v.55-7) seems inconsequential fooling until we jump to the concealed pun on *weed*; Olivia will lay aside her mourning for her brother as quickly as a widow is supposed to shed her weeds, since she shares with all the characters in the play the knowledge that the rose must be plucked 'whilest yet is time'. There is less delicate wit in an obscure passage of Hal's railing at Poins in *Henry IV* part 2 but the lines deserve comment here because editors have generally missed both the spoken and unspoken puns. The tennis-court keeper, says Hal, knows the inventory of Poins' shirts.

> for it is a low ebbe of Linnen with thee, when thou kept'st not *Racket* there, as thou hast not done a great while, because the rest of thy *Low Countries*, haue made a *shift* to eate vp thy *Holland*: and God knows whether those that *bal* out the ruines of thy linnen shal inherite his kingdom: but the Midwiues say, the children are not in the *fault* wherevpon the world increases, and kinreds are mightily strengthened.[1] (II.ii.22-31)

Hal's insinuation, that Poins' linen has all gone to clothe his bastard children, is made in a double sequence of puns: *racket*, *ball* and *fault* derive from the tennis-court, and the quibbles in *shift* and *Holland* are sustained, as M. R. Ridley has shown,[2]

---

[1] Quoted from the *Variorum* edition of M. A. Shaaber, pp. 135-6. The words 'and God . . . strengthened' are not in the Folio.

[2] *New Temple Shakespeare, 2 Henry IV*, p. 145.

by an unspoken pun on *piece-makers*, which gives rise to the echo of the Beatitudes in 'shall inherit his kingdom'.

One other kind of mainly unconscious wordplay claims notice here. 'The meaning of a word on some occasions', writes I. A. Richards, 'is quite as much in what it keeps out, or at a distance, as in what it brings in.'[1] Shakespeare's words often carry an impossible and so negative meaning which acts as a deep shadow to make the dominant significance more brilliant. If the negative meaning is, in other contexts, the more usual one, there is a split-second hesitation in reading which lends piquancy to the phrase as it is finally understood. The impossible sense of 'candid' highlights Hamlet's 'No, let the Candied tongue lick[2] absurd pompe' (III.ii.65). 'Ciuill Butchery' (*I Henry IV*, I.i.13) and 'ruthfull butchery' (*Richard III*, IV.iii.5) gain vigour from the negative and rejected meanings 'polite' and 'pitying'. And the phrase 'Rumour . . . is of so easie, and so plaine a stop' in the Induction to *Henry IV* part 2 stays in our mind because Rumour is the one thing that cannot be brought to a stop in the commonest sense of the word.

At this point, when our analysis of Shakespeare's verbal associations is in danger of becoming over-subtle, it is as well to remind ourselves that the critical value of this kind of investigation is limited. It tells us a certain amount about the poetic process in general. By strengthening our recognition of the fact that poetic thought is always verbal, it may safeguard us from any tendency to treat language as the dress rather than the substance of poetry. It can also throw light on the creative process in certain other poets, such as Hopkins, who have the same strong bent as Shakespeare for verbal association through assonance. And we have already seen how serviceable it can be to the editor in deciding whether or not to embark on emendation. It has one further practical use: it can strengthen the case for or against the inclusion of a play in the Shakespeare canon, for once we have grown accustomed to Shakespeare's verbal habits the absence of any one of them from a play casts doubt upon his authorship. The parts of *Henry VIII* held to be

[1] I. A. Richards, *op. cit.*, p. 63. See also Margaret Schlauch, *The Gift of Tongues* (1943), pp. 122-3.   [2] For Folio *like*.

non-Shakespearean contain remarkably few puns, except for some *double-entendres* which do not recur among the Folio plays. On the other hand, the second and third parts of *Henry VI* have some passages where the images are mortised by puns in the real Shakespearean manner. In the first scene of part 2, Gloucester begins to vent his feelings on the marriage alliance with France in the words

> Braue *Peeres* of England, Pillars of the State,
> To you Duke Humfrey must vnload his greefe . . .
>
> (I.i.76-7)

Nothing could be more Shakespearean than the way *Peers* (in the sense of noblemen) here evokes the double image of *piers* as pillars and of the piers or jetties at which boats are unladed. It is difficult, therefore, to reject this as 'incongruous imagery' as Dr Wilson has done in his New Cambridge edition. In part 3, Dr Wilson even feels that Richard's fine soliloquy in the third act is basically the work of another dramatist, probably Greene; but if this is so, the revision by Shakespeare must have been drastic to give such typical linkage of ideas through word-play as the following:

> Ile make my Heauen, to dreame vpon the Crowne,
> And whiles I liue, t'account this World but Hell,
> Vntill my mis-shap'd *Trunke*, that beares this Head,
> Be round impaled with a glorious Crowne.
> And yet I know not how to get the Crowne,
> For many Liues stand betweene me and home:
> And I, like one lost in a Thornie Wood,
> That rents the Thornes, and is rent with the Thornes,
>
> .   .   .   .   .
>
> Torment my selfe, to catch the English Crowne:
> And from that torment I will free my selfe,
> Or hew my way out with a bloody Axe.
>
> (III.ii.168-81)

Trunk begins a tree image sustained through *crown* ('the leafy head of a tree or shrub'—*N.E.D.*) and the simile of the thorny wood; but the meaning of 'body' is not relinquished and gives rise to a grim image at the end of the quotation. Richard will have Henry's crown even if he has to cut his head from his body as one would hew a tree's crown from its trunk. Although the passage is decked out with rhetorical figures of words, learnt from Marlowe and others, its deeper organisation is like that of the verse in any of Shakespeare's better authenticated plays.

Just because this associative use of wordplay is so personal a feature of Shakespeare's style, its study brings the interpretative critic onto dangerous ground. It is fatally easy here to fall into the 'personal heresy' of substituting an amateur psycho-analysis of the writer for a critical analysis of the work. But over and above their personal nature of a poetic signature, Shakespeare's puns have an active dramatic function which is very much the critic's concern. They may be 'in character' or they may be a vital part of the play's thought. Both these functions will repay investigation.

3

'Well, your old vice still: mistake the word', complains Speed to Launce. Launce not only keeps his old vice, he *is* the old Vice, the professional funny man whose comic turns break the illusion of *Two Gentlemen of Verona* as completely as the illusion of pantomime is shattered by the Dame's antics. His remonstrance with his dog Crab is a good music-hall act, and there is the laboured, hard-driven wordplay of such turns in all his punning: 'I (a lost-Mutton) gaue your Letter to her (a lac'd-Mutton) and she (a lac'd-Mutton) gaue mee (a lost-Mutton) nothing for my labour' (I.i.101-4). However Shakespeare might feel about the extra-dramatic role of the clown, the company had clowns and the public expected to be entertained by them. Lancelot Gobbo, in *The Merchant of Venice*, is still the old Vice whose quibbles bore Lorenzo: 'How euerie foole can play vpon the word.' In the end, Shakespeare found various ways to reconcile his artistic conscience with the demands of his audience. When he keeps clownish quibbles, such as those in the opening scene of *Julius Cæsar*, they are made to fulfil a dramatic purpose: in this case, they tune up the audience's responsiveness to words to the pitch at which Marullus's outburst of rhetoric gains the greatest possible effect. Or the quibbling jester may be transformed into a Fool whose wit is 'not altogether Foole', or who is, like Feste, not a Fool but a corrupter of words. Both Lear's Fool and Olivia's corrupt words in a way that brings out the underlying themes of each play. Shakespeare had one other device for keeping the wordplay which delighted his audience and himself, without breaking the dramatic illusion, and that was to develop the contrast, first shown in *Love's Labour's Lost*, between the simpletons, who are at the mercy of words they do not fully understand, and the sophisticated wits, who show their mastery of words by ringing all possible changes on their meanings. In this way Shakespeare's comic puns, from being the wisecracks of an intrusive clown, are transformed into puns of character.

A very thorough revelation of character can be made in a pun. Time and again the wordplay of Shakespeare's personages lends support to Freud's contention that the function of verbal wit is to afford a safe outlet for repressed impulses. The impulse to be irrational gives us the type of harmless, pointless punning represented by Beatrice's '*ciuill* as an Orange', in which our pleasure comes from the verbal ingenuity itself, and the impulses to be aggressive, exhibitionist or sceptical give us pointed, tendentious puns which please speaker and hearer because they act as a safety valve for these anti-social instincts. In good company—which means tolerant, congenial company, which will not be critical of our absurdity nor shocked by the disclosure of normally-inhibited feelings—we pun freely and intentionally. The mood is one of self-possession; we feel no need to conceal, either from ourselves or others, what we are in every part of our disposition. Such company, in Shakespeare, may be found in Eastcheap. Falstaff, whose very charm lies in the way he represents freedom from all the normal inhibitions, even succeeds in breaking down those of the Lord Chief Justice, that walking embodiment of Freud's Censor, to the point where he, too, begins to pun.

This wordplay of good company is sometimes quite untendentious, an overflow of spirits in which the desire to talk sheer disconnected nonsense is satisfied at the same time as reason is appeased by the verbal connections between the topics.[1] There is not much meaning but a good deal of exuberance in Romeo's interchange of puns with Mercutio the night after the ball. 'Oh here's a wit of Cheuerell', exclaims Mercutio, 'that stretches from an ynch narrow, to an ell broad' (II.iv.90-1); and from this point the jests also broaden. For, as Viola says to Feste when he too (of all people) complains that a sentence is 'but a cheu'rill gloue to a good wit'[2]: 'they that dally nicely with words may quickly make them wanton'. Most of the witty wordplay in Shakespeare is either wanton or aggressive. The liveliest exchanges are between those pairs of lovers who fight their way to the altar, for their wordplay is doubly tendentious in being at once both hostile and seductive. The rough-and-tumble exchanges between Katherine and Petruchio, or the more stylish repartee of Rosaline and Berowne, and of Beatrice and Benedick, gain from this wordplay a truth to life not found among the bickerings of Congreve's lovers, whose Augustan wit gives no countenance to the quibble.

Tendentious verbal wit can be sinister as well as comic. The battle of wit between the sexes, which affords much of the laughter in Shakespeare's comedies, is fought out with savage fury by Richard and Anne in the first scene of *Richard III.* As a complete egotist—'I am my selfe alone'—Richard is an exception to the general rule that tendentious wordplay is a game for two or more players, since A's insinuations must be understood by B, even though he pretend not to recognise the *double-entendre.* But Richard takes a solitary pleasure in his wordplay at Clarence's expense; and Buckingham, when he equivocates with the doomed Hastings, shows himself in this, as in everything else, a pale imitation of Richard. It more commonly happens that the aggressive meaning of a word is the blade that strikes home, while the attacker shields himself

[1] Freud's contention (see *Wit and the Unconscious,* trans. A. A. Brill, (1922), pp. 190-213) that punning releases a desire to talk nonsense which was suppressed in the nursery gains support from the experimental psychologists, who have shown that in the process of verbal association children generalise by homophones (*style* to *stile*) more easily than grown-ups, who prefer semantic generalisation (*style* to *fashion*). Perhaps the Victorians were ashamed of puns because they had received an ultra-rational education from the English Rousseauists who tried to 'inculcate the principles of Reason and Morality' at a tender age. Puns let us be unprincipled about both.　　　　　　　　　　　[2] For Folio *twitte.*

behind its innocuous meaning. Macduff makes use of this kind of ambiguity when he tries to rouse Malcolm to the counter-attack:

> Bleed, bleed poore Country,
> Great Tyrrany, lay thou thy basis sure,
> For goodnesse dare not check thee: wear thou[1] thy wrongs,
> The Title, is *affear'd*.   (IV.iii.31-4)

The defensive meaning here is *affeered*—'assured, confirmed'—but in the aggressive meaning 'affeared' lies Macduff's insinuation that Malcolm is afraid to assert his right to the Scottish throne. Another use of wordplay observed by Freud, that of an outlet for scepticism about authority, is found whenever a character uses a double meaning conspiratorially, in order to sound another character's disaffection. The most striking example occurs in *Richard II* when, after the death of Gaunt, Northumberland, Ross and Willoughby probe each other's thoughts about the imminent return of Bolingbroke.[2]

Hostile wordplay gains from having a stage audience to appreciate its edge. Fabian speaks of Sir Andrew's 'dormouse valour' (*Twelfth Night*, III.ii.22), knowing that if Sir Andrew, whose head has scarcely room for one meaning at a time, understands anything by the phrase it will be 'dormant'; but Sir Toby is present to relish the joke. In other plays the puns at the expense of a third person are socially exclusive, and imply: 'You and I understand this, but he doesn't, because he doesn't belong to our set.' This is never an attractive form of wit, and when Shakespeare uses it in the final interlude scenes of *Love's Labour's Lost* and *A Midsummer Night's Dream* our sympathies veer round to protest with Holofernes that 'this is not generous, not gentle, not humble'. Perhaps the excuse can be made for each set of rather callow wits that their self-esteem is badly in need of compensation. The Athenian lovers have been made to look pretty fools by Puck, whereas not even bewitchment could make an ass of Bottom; and the courtiers of Navarre have been well flouted in their own masque before they begin to jeer at the efforts of Armado and

---

[1] For Folio $\frac{u}{y}$ [2] See below, p. 82

his friends. Such punning is at any rate relaxed and good-humoured by comparison with that found in another triangular verbal situation, the 'volley of words' between Sylvia's two suitors in her presence (*Two Gentlemen*, II.iv), which has the double purpose of venting the hostility of each to the other and of showing off the wit of each to Sylvia. The grimmest hostile wordplay of all is to be found in the double-tongued subtleties of Westmoreland and Prince John when they lure the rebels into their trap in the second part of *Henry IV*. Westmoreland drinks to the rebel Archbishop with the words:

> I pledge your Grace:
> And if you knew what *paines* I haue bestow'd,
> To breede this present Peace,
> You would drinke freely: but my loue to ye,
> Shall shew it selfe more openly hereafter,
>
> (IV.ii.73-6)

where, in addition to the ambiguity of 'my love to ye', *pains* has the proleptic meaning of 'punishment' as well as that of 'efforts'; and just before the rebels are arrested John quibbles again in the phrase: 'I trust (Lords) wee shall *lye* to night together', since the rebels will not lodge with him but lie in prison or perhaps in 'Treasons true Bed', the grave. Since it is difficult to believe that Shakespeare condones John's Machiavellian *lies*, I suspect that he here adds his own ironic wordplay to that of the character.

Another psychological function of wordplay which everyone has witnessed or experienced is its use to gain relief from a state of emotional tension. Shakespeare knew about this as early as the date he wrote *Two Gentlemen of Verona*, where Julia twice employs puns to this end. On the first occasion, her maid Lucetta produces a letter from Proteus. Julia suppresses with a tantrum her strong desire to read it, and then gives vent to her disturbed feelings in a volley of puns—which incidentally illustrate Shakespeare's detailed technical knowledge of music.[1] A similar incident occurs in the fourth act of the play when Julia, disguised as a youth, hears Proteus courting Sylvia. Examples crowd to mind of characters in later plays who

[1] I.ii.80 ff. See Edward W. Naylor: *Shakespeare and Music* (1896), pp. 26-7.

unpack their hearts with double meanings. At the near-tragic climax of *Much Ado*, when Hero has been rejected at the altar, Beatrice quibbles with Benedick before she brings herself to declare her love for him and to demand vengeance on Claudio. Hamlet lets off flashes of wordplay in the thunderous atmosphere of the Play Scene, and once his plot to catch the conscience of the King has succeeded he gives his triumphant feelings vent in a topical flight full of puns. Lear's Fool tries by punning to relax the tension of his master's thoughts; but because such relief cannot come from another, his quibbles only act as an irritant to Lear's imagination. Finally, there is the explosive wordplay through which Leontes' jealousy erupts in the first act of *The Winter's Tale*.

Johnson was scandalised by the untimeliness of many of Shakespeare's puns. For a character to quibble in the teeth of death, as many do in the plays, was contrary to 'reason, propriety and truth'. Yet he seldom fails to recognise such a pun when it occurs. He sees, and deplores, the wordplay of the captive Posthumous:

> and so great Powres,
> If you will take this Audit, take this life,
> And cancell these *cold Bonds*, (V.iv.26-8)

and unlike the Victorian editors, he does not try to exculpate Henry IV from punning in the line 'England shall double *gild* thy treble gilt'. But it was inconceivable to Johnson that sick men could in fact play so nicely with words. Yet if, with Coleridge, we reject the Augustan theory of literary 'decorum', of life-as-it-should-be, and again consider how and when people pun in life-as-it-is, we find plenty of death-bed quibbles. Keats, on his arrival in Italy, 'summoned up more puns, in a sort of desperation, in one week than in any year of my life'. A generation earlier, Danton had silenced a fellow-victim of the Terror with a most Shakespearean pun: 'Plus de vers! Dans huit jours, tu en feras assez.' There is the same *panache* in the last speeches of many Shakespearean characters: in King John's reply to the question 'How fares your Maiesty?'—'Poison'd, ill *fare*'; or, in the same play, in the dying Melun's warning to the English barons:

Euen this ill night, your breathing shall expire,
Paying the *fine* of rated Treachery,
Euen with a treacherous *fine* of all your liues.

(V.iv.36-8)

But there is more than bravado in Antonio's words as he
prepares to let Shylock have his bond: 'Ile pay it instantly,
with *all my heart*' (IV.i.282). Here, although in a serio-comic
context, we recognise magnanimity, the self-possession of a
whole mind with which such tragic heroes as Romeo and Hamlet
meet their deaths, and proclaim in a quibble their reconciliation
to themselves and their destiny.

All the wordplay of character examined so far has been witty
and intentional. Shakespeare also makes his characters speak unconscious puns, which reveal their inmost feelings exactly in the
way that people's wishes are exposed by a slip of the tongue or
of the pen. By selecting a word with a secondary meaning, the
speaker allows himself—or more frequently, herself—the oppor-
tunity to say something which caution or modesty withholds
from direct expression. Thus, when King John's barons are protesting against his second coronation, Salisbury says:

To this effect, before you were new crown'd
We breath'd our Councell: but it pleas'd your Highnes
To ouer-beare it, and we are all well pleas'd,
Since all, and euery part of what we would
Doth *make a stand*, at what your Highnesse will.

(IV.ii.35-9)

If *stand* means withdrawal or cessation, this is a most dutiful
speech, but it may equally well mean a defensive stance, and
this is what Salisbury would like it to mean. In fact the ambiguity may not be merely Salisbury's unconscious release of
his defiance; it is just possible that it is a deliberately aggressive
piece of quibbling, a veiled threat. Henry VI, however, is not a
character who is likely to devise deliberate equivocations, and
his words after the death of Gloucester unintentionally give
away his confused feelings:

O thou that iudgest all things, *stay* my thoghts:
My thoughts, that labour to perswade my soule,
Some violent hands were laid on Humfries life:

If my suspect be false, forgiue me God,
For iudgement onely doth belong to thee.

(Part 2, III.ii.136-40)

It is not easy here to decide which is the uppermost and conscious meaning of *stay*. Does Henry pray God to strengthen and support his detection of the murder, while unconsciously the meaning 'stop' betrays his reluctance to take any steps towards retribution? Or does he seemingly pray for his evil suspicions to be checked and prevented, while unconsciously he seeks support for his conviction that Gloucester has been murdered? The uncertainty itself reveals the vacillations of mind that make decisive action impossible for Henry. One further example from the Histories is to be found in the great scene of *Henry IV* part 1 between the king and his son. Henry reproaches Hal for cheapening his presence in vulgar company:

> Had I so lauish of my presence beene,
> So common hackney'd in the eyes of men,
> So stale and cheape to vulgar Company;
> Opinion, that did helpe me to the Crowne,
> Had still kept loyall to possession,
> And left me in reputelesse banishment,
> A fellow of no *marke*, nor likelyhood.

(III.ii.39-45)

While the superficial meaning of this presents Henry's advancement to the throne as something good and desirable, the emotional counterstress of 'loyal' suggests that Henry cannot free himself from the usurper's burden of guilt. This undercurrent of meaning persists in *mark*. Because Henry feels himself marked out for the vengeance of Heaven (and the word is used in this sense earlier in the same scene), the line 'A fellow of no marke, nor likelyhood' is ambivalent in its blend of self-gratulation with the remorse that darkens the whole reign of Henry IV.

Shakespeare's heroines afford the best examples of this kind of unintentional wordplay. This we might expect. Women are more inhibited than men by social conventions, especially by the convention that makes man the pursuer and women the reluctant quarry. It is true that such a convention does not much

35

hamper the speech of such great ladies as Olivia and Portia, but Portia's spontaneous feelings are kept effectively in check by her vow to marry none but the suitor who chooses the right casket. 'So is the *will* of a liuing daughter curb'd by the *will* of a dead father.' It sounds a case for the psycho-analysts, and in fact Freud took one of his best examples of a revealing slip of the tongue from Portia's speech to Bassanio:

> One halfe of me is yours, the other halfe yours,
> Mine owne I would say.   (III.ii.16-17)

The same scene between Bassanio and Portia affords a good example of the kind of *double-entendre* by which a character may unconsciously allow a voice to strong feelings. As Bassanio is on the point of opening the right casket, Portia exclaims:

> O loue be moderate, allay thy extasie,
> In *measure raine* thy ioy, scant this excesse.   (111-12)

'Rein' is the dominant, external meaning, but Portia, no longer curbed by the conditions of her father's will, is about to open a floodgate of delight, and this gives us the meaning 'rain' while 'reign' is also suggested by her triumph at her lover's choice; and *measure* implies both moderation and its reverse—a generous allowance, the sort of measure which is pressed down and running over, as well as the lively rhythm to which Portia's heart is dancing.[1]

Whereas Portia, the golden fleece of Belmont, is a prize sought by many adventurers, Hellena, in *All's Well*, has to pursue a man who scorns her poverty and low birth. Her soliloquy in the first scene is an interesting reversal of the more usual linguistic situation in which a woman who must feign 'daunger' and indifference allows her real inclination to reveal itself through the wordplay:

> Th'ambition in my loue thus plagues it selfe:
> The *hind* that would be *mated* by the Lion
> Must die for loue. 'Twas prettie, though a plague

---

[1] Compare the end of *As You Like It*:
   Play Musicke, and you Brides and Bride-groomes all,
   With measure heap'd in ioy, to th' Measures fall.   (V.iv.185-6)

To see him euerie houre to sit and *draw*
His *arched* browes, his hawking eie, his curles
In our hearts table: *heart* too capeable
Of euerie *line* and *tricke* of his sweet *fauour*.

(I.i.102-8)

Hind, which has the subordinate meaning of 'a menial', here gives rise to the theme of hunting, which implies that in Hellena's fantasies the conventional relationship is restored to make Bertram the hunter and herself the hunted. This theme is sustained in *draw* ('to draw a bow' as well as 'to depict'), by *arched* which produces a faint reverberation of *bows* in *brows* (eyebrows are bow-shaped), and by the way *heart* echoes *hind* and so suggests 'hart'. So in the next verse, *line* implies not only 'outline of a drawing' but also, by proximity with the ideas of hunting and hawking, and with *mated* which can have the sense of 'trapped' (as at chess), a fishing line: 'Bertram ought to be angling for *me*'. *Trick*, besides meaning 'character-istic expression' and 'delineation' suggests 'the amorous guile with which Bertram ought to pursue *me*' (compare Parolles' 'Trickes hee hath had in him, which Gentlemen haue' V.iii.241-2 with reference to Bertram's wooing of Diana). *Favour* in addition to 'appearance' means 'the token one lover gives another and which Bertram ought to give *me*'—a meaning prepared by an earlier use of *favour*, impelled perhaps by the same wishful thinking, in this same speech:

My imagination
Carries no *fauour* in't but Bertrams.

If the individual fragments of this wordplay seem microscopi-cally small, they add up to something easily visible, and we must be grateful for this indication that Hellena has her proper pride, and is not after all entirely satisfied with her role of Patient Griselda. In the same way, we are delighted when Miranda reveals a mind of her own in telling her father that Ferdinand is '*gentle* and not *fearful*' (I.ii.465). Ostensibly this means: 'He is harmless and gives no one cause to fear him', but over and above this Miranda, who has found a new loyalty, is saying: 'You need not think that he is afraid of you because, out of pure good breeding, he puts up patiently with your ill-treatment.' Juliet's growth of character is likewise marked by wordplay,[1] but Miranda's is the more attractive because it has the air of being entirely unconscious.

Shakespeare's own poetic habit of linking disparate images through wordplay is sometimes transferred to his personages as an indication of character. It is, of course, difficult to separate Shakespeare's own practice as a poet from the mental processes he attributes to his characters, but some verbal associations of this kind are more dramatic, more 'in character' than others. In the following passage, the wordplay, which for the most part is involuntary and works below the level of consciousness, is in a sense Macbeth's own:

> Be innocent of the knowledge, dearest Chuck,
> Till thou applaud the *deed*: Come, *seeling* Night,
> Skarfe vp the tender Eye of pittifull Day,
> And with thy bloodie and inuisible Hand
> Cancell and teare to pieces that great *Bond*,
> Which keepes me *pale*. Light thickens,
> And the Crow makes Wing to th' Rookie Wood.
> (III.ii.45-51)

The wordplay here starts with a quibble on *deed* in the sense of an action and of a legal document. To applaud a deed in this second sense is to set one's seal to it; but *sealing* night turns into night *seeling*, or sewing day's eyelids as a falconer might a bird's, through association with the winged creatures—bats and beetles—of Macbeth's previous speech, and with the oddly inappropriate 'Chuck'. The legal deed, momentarily submerged, reappears in the great *Bond*, which in its turn has been suggested by Lady Macbeth's previous words about Banquo and Fleance: 'But in them, Natures Coppie's not eterne'. A *bond* is also something that constrains, as does a *pale*, or fence; if the stronger meaning of *pale* as 'colourless' is reflected in 'Light thickens', the meaning of a fence (as in Autolycus's punning song: 'For the red blood raigns in the winters pale') helps to

[1] See below, p. 71. Lieutenant Lismahago paraphrased it: 'being gentle, that is, *high spirited*, he won't tamely bear an insult'. See *Humphry Clinker*, (1771), II.182.

bring us to the crow which ignores fences as the crow flies. These involved puns are an index to Macbeth's complex turmoil of feelings, which include fear, weariness, and the deliberate suppression of tender misgivings. The great bond may be the witches' promise to Banquo, which causes Macbeth to fear assassination, or it may be the bond of nature between himself and Banquo which his fear compels him to break. If it is the bond of life given to Banquo by Nature, we are impelled to ask why it should be a bond, rather than the more common lease of life, until we see that for Macbeth life has become bondage and that he is 'cabin'd, crib'd, confin'd' in the consequences of Duncan's murder.

In the ramblings of the drunken porter, *Macbeth* furnishes another vivid example of the free association of ideas through unconscious wordplay. The Porter begins his devil-portering by admitting a farmer to Hell, and then, perhaps because 'Farmer' was one of the aliases of the Jesuit Henry Garnet, as his recent trial had brought to light, he adds an equivocator. Next comes a tailor, whose association with *Hell* probably lay in the fact that a tailor's discard, where he threw odd scraps of cloth, was so called. The whole Porter scene is an illustration of the kind of wordplay, conscious or unconscious, which results when the mental censor, whose job is to eliminate the illogical and improper meanings of words, temporarily leaves his post. If the censor decamps altogether, the result is the wordplay of insanity, such as is displayed in Lear's uncontrolled stream of verbal associations:

> No, they cannot touch me for *coining*[1]. I am the King himselfe . . . Nature's aboue Art, in that respect. Ther's your *Presse-money*. That fellow handles his bow like a Crow-keeper: draw mee a Cloathiers yard. Looke, looke, a Mouse: peace, *peace*, this *peece* of toasted Cheese will doo't. There's my Gauntlet, Ile proue it on a Gyant. Bring vp the browne *Billes*. O well flowne Bird: i'th'clout, i'th'clout.   (IV.vi.84-94)

This is a long way from nonsense. Deliberate, literary Nonsense deals in isolated units, even dissociating things which are nearly identical ('plenty of money wrapped up in a five-pound

[1] For the Folio *crying*. The Quarto has *coining*.

note'), whereas in the seeming nonsense of madness there are clear connections both of sense and sound. When Otway's mad heroine speaks of 'Lutes, laurels, seas of milk, and ships of amber', the poet, by giving rein to his fancy, has produced a line organised into an Augustan neatness; the first two and the last two items are firmly paired both in sound (by alliteration) and in meaning (Apollo's music and laurel wreath; ships on the sea). Coleridge, bent on proving that fancy, unlike imagination, presents an unorganised medley to the mind, unconsciously tried to make Otway's line more chaotic by quoting it as 'Lutes, lobsters, seas of milk, and ships of amber', but even so he could not achieve the perfect dissociation of the professional nonsense writer; lobsters go with lutes by alliteration and with seas and ships in association of ideas.[1] To write without any meaning requires considerable rational effort. The poet and the psychologist both know that madness is full of meaning, that the puns of mania or the portmanteau words of the schizophrenic are the outer verbal evidence of a strong underlying association of ideas. So in this passage Lear's *coining* fuses the idea of begetting children, over whom he should have parental authority, with the idea of the royal prerogative, of which he has now been deprived by his rebellious daughters; and *press-money*, in the sense of the king's shilling, follows from the coining image, not only because of the pun on (im)*press*, but also because Lear, struggling to assert the authority which makes him every inch a king, imagines he is reviewing his bowmen. The silence in which the imaginary marksman takes aim is one of those still intervals in Lear's storm of feeling when he struggles to find patience: 'Grant me patience, patience 'tis I need'. Momentarily he has enough to tame a mouse, but it gives way at once to a challenging defiance, to a fresh assertion of the power and authority he has actually lost, in 'Bring up the brown Billes'; and then the alternative meaning of *bill*, together with Lear's fresh gust of anger, release the bowman's arrow in flight: 'Oh, well flowne Bird'.

[1] See Elizabeth Sewell, *The Field of Nonsense* (1952), and for Coleridge, *Biographia Literaria*, ed. Shawcross, I.62, and Livingston Lowes, *The Road to Xanadu* (1951), pp. 346-7.

4

In discussing the truth to life of Shakespeare's puns, I have spoken of certain of them as 'unconscious'. This is a misleading term. A Shakespearean character can have no unconscious mind, since it lacks the racial, pre-natal and infantile memories with which the unconscious is stored. Criticism which probes the unconscious mind of Lear or of Leontes is only a modern refinement of the fallacy which led earlier critics to speculate about Lear's wife, Lady Macbeth's children and Hamlet's studies at Wittenberg. When the dramatist holds the mirror up to nature, it is naivety to peer behind it to see what is through the looking-glass. There is only a reflecting surface: only words given to an actor to help him impersonate a character in action. But the reflecting surface gives the illusion of a third dimension, and the wordplay of Shakespeare's characters seems to stem from the sources of wordplay in real life. Only when we look behind the mirror for those sources we find—Shakespeare. The vital wordplay in Shakespeare's writings is that between the characters and their creator, between the primary meanings of words in the context of a person's speech and their secondary meanings as part of the play's underlying pattern of thought. The chief function of the pun is to connect subject and object, inner force with outer form, the poetic vision with the characters in action that are its theatrical embodiment. The play's the thing—not the elusive mind of the playwright nor the illusory minds of his characters.

Wordplay is one of the most effective means towards the ironic interplay between character and creator which is the essence of drama. It may be anticipatory or retrospective, may imply a difference of values between what the speaker is allowed to say for himself and what the writer and his audience think, or it may simply intensify or widen the speaker's meaning to give it significance beyond the moment of speech. The only wordplay of this type in Shakespeare which is quite unsuccessful is the comic kind—for example, the dismal humour of the scene in French between Alice and Katherine in *Henry V*. The similar Latin *viva* of little William in *The Merry Wives of*

Windsor is much better comedy, because the audience is not left to supply the *double-entendres* for itself but enjoys the mingled pride and disapproval with which William's mother listens to her son's display of book-learning. But, by and large, the best comic puns in Shakespeare are in character and the best ironic ones are uncomic.

New examples of anticipatory irony through wordplay emerge at every performance of a Shakespearean play. There is an instance in the third act of *Richard III*, when Hastings spurns Stanley's warning messages with the words:

> Goe, bid thy Master rise, and come to me,
> And we will both together to the Tower,
> Where he shall see the Bore will vse vs *kindly*.
>
> (III.ii.31-3)

We know here that Richard will in fact use Hastings *kindly*— that is, according to his savage nature; we have just heard him decide to 'chop off his head'. The audience has been more subtly prepared to taste the irony in a speech by the Princess in *Love's Labour's Lost*, when the King of Navarre tries to prevent her entry to his palace:

Nau. Heare me deare Lady, I haue sworne an oath.
Prin. Our Lady helpe my Lord, he'll be forsworne.
Nau. Not for the world faire Madam, by my will.
Prin. Why, *will* shall breake it *will*, and nothing else.[1]

> (II.i.97-100)

The Princess presumably means by *will* 'volition' or 'resolution' —which is the sense in which the King has just used the word. But Berowne's scepticism over the King's oath of celibacy ('For euery man with his affects is borne') has prepared us to take *will* in the sense of 'affects' and more particularly of 'sexual desire', which in the punning Sonnets is constantly at variance with the Will as a faculty; and this ironic meaning is justified by the end of the play, when will, in the sense of 'affects' has broken down all barriers of resolution between the lords and the ladies. Some of the ironic equivocations in

---

[1] Capell punctuates: 'will shall break it: will and nothing else' and my explanation follows this reading.

Othello are apparent on a first hearing; for example, Othello's ominous thanks to Iago: 'I am *bound* to you for euer.' But only when we know that the secondary Elizabethan meaning of *conveyance* is 'trickery' ('Conueyers are you all' says the deposed Richard), can we feel the tragic irony in Othello's praise of Iago before the Senate:

> A man he is of honesty and trust:
> To his *conueyance* I assigne my wife.   (I.iii.286-7)

Certain words with contradictory meanings lend themselves most readily to this anticipatory irony. The verb *seem* and the noun or adjective *seeming* can imply either display or deception,[1] and in the last act of *Henry IV* part 1 the word is subtly used in this double sense. Worcester returns from his audience with Henry and tells Hotspur: 'There is no seeming mercy in the King' (V.ii.34). Worcester is withholding the King's offer of an amnesty because he believes it fraudulent, a *seeming* mercy, and this gives his words a negative dramatic irony. They gain also a positive irony from the audience's belief that the king's offer is sincere; Worcester is more right than he knows, since the king's mercy is not seeming but genuine. Even more subtle is Lear's use of the same word when he offers the dowerless Cordelia to Burgundy:

> If ought within that little *seeming* substance,
> Or all of it with our displeasure piec'd,
> And nothing more may fitly like your Grace,
> Shee's there, and she is yours.   (I.i.201-4)

Lear's praise is capable of many interpretations according to whether we read 'little-seeming substance', 'little seeming-substance' or 'little, seeming substance', and according to the meaning we put on *seeming*. At the simplest interpretation, Lear is saying: 'She is not much to look at', but because we know, or guess, how little seeming there is in Cordelia by comparison with her sisters, we feel the anticipatory irony of his words, an irony all the more sharp if Lear himself is being ironic and means: 'This genuine creature who refuses to flatter'

---

[1] As in *Lucrece*, 600-1; Sonnet 102; *Much Ado*, IV.i.55-6; *Hamlet*, III.ii.92; *Measure for Measure*, II.iv.15; *Othello*, I.iii.109; III.i.126.

(Muir). The close dramatic irony of the other great tragedies is helped at every turn by wordplay. Duncan's 'It is a *peerlesse* kinsman' prepares us for Macbeth's refusal to remain a thane among thanes. Only a monarch is literally peerless. *Antony and Cleopatra* is exceptional among the tragedies in having very few ambiguities. The reason is perhaps that the chief characters are masters of their own fate and know the scope and consequence of their actions as well as we do in the audience. Enobarbus is the only character who lacks self-knowledge; and his disloyalty is ironically presaged in his reply to Antony's 'Woo't thou fight well?'—'Ile *strike* and cry, *Take all*' (IV.ii.8). *Strike* can mean 'lower sail' as well as 'hit', and *take all* is a cry of surrender as well as a cry of 'No composition'.

Irony may thus be used to weld the parts of a play together. It can also convey a critical undertone by suggesting a difference of values between the poet and the character animated by the poetry. A non-Shakespearean example of such irony is offered by Volpone's temptation of Corvino's wife:

> A diamant, would haue bought Lollia Pavlina,
> When she came in, like star-light, hid with iewels
> That were the spoiles of prouinces.
>
> > (*Volpone*, III.vii.195-7)

The suggestion of prostitution in *bought*, of brutal waste in *spoils of provinces*, and of vulgar, unnatural ostentation contrasted with the natural beauty of starlight in *hid with jewels*, set up a powerful countercurrent to the seductive rhetoric of Volpone's words. Shakespeare does just the same thing when he makes Troilus declare that Helen's beauty 'makes stale the morning'; the lifeless hyperbole redounds to the discredit of Helen and expresses the Trojan weariness with a ten-year war fought about 'a cuckold and a whore'. Helen, whom Troilus goes on to compare to an inestimable pearl, is in fact no more to be valued than the gems which lie on the seabed in Clarence's dream:

> Me thoughts, I saw a thousand fearfull wrackes:
> A thousand men that Fishes gnaw'd vpon:
> Wedges of Gold, great Anchors, heapes of Pearle,
> *Inestimable* Stones, *vnvalewed* Iewels,

All scattred in the bottome of the Sea,
Some lay in dead-mens Sculles, and in the holes
Where eyes did once inhabit, there were crept
(As 'twere in scorne of eyes) reflecting Gemmes,
That woo'd the slimy bottome of the deepe
And mock'd the dead bones that lay scattred by.

(*Richard III*, I.iv.24-33)

The image of the gems for eyes, and the ambiguity of *inestimable* and *unvalued*, work together. The jewels which once seemed beyond price to their owners are now as worthless to them, being dead, as their glitter is a vain substitute for the living eye. Exactly the opposite effect is achieved in *Pericles*, when Cerimon revives the seemingly dead Thaisa:

The Diamonds
of a most praysed *water* doth appeare
To make the world twise rich, (III.ii.102-3)

for *wáter* suggests the life-giving sea whose currents, under the guidance of the play's presiding deity Diana, restore lost treasures to the old king. One further instance of a shift of values conveyed through a shift in meaning occurs when Antonio retorts to Shylock's account of how Jacob's flock multiplied: 'This was a *venture* sir that Iacob seru'd for.' The nuance is not great here between the ostensible meaning of *venture*—'a course or proceeding the outcome of which is uncertain, but which is attended by the risk of danger or loss' (*N.E.D.* 4) and the underlying meaning of 'a commercial enterprise' (*N.E.D.* 5), but it is sufficient momentarily to bring Antonio's ventures as a merchant under the same scrutiny as Shylock's dealings as a moneylender. Marlowe or Jonson would have made the comparison more pointed, more satirical; Shakespeare uses it only to flash a brief light on the conduct of the Gentiles before he returns to the iniquities of the Jew.

Sometimes an isolated pun offers much more than this flicker of light; it can be the lightning flash that illumines a whole play. Immediately before he kills Desdemona, Othello cries 'O periur'd woman, thou do'st *stone* my heart', and because we take *stone* in the sense of 'strike, batter' as well as that of 'petrify' our pity here keeps even with our terror in a perfect tragic equilibrium. Similar power in a very simple phrase is found in Gloucester's words to the Old Man who has led him to Edgar disguised as Poor Tom:

> And bring some couering for this naked *Soule*
> Which Ile intreate to leade me.   (*King Lear*, IV.i.44–5)

Soul has the double meaning of 'person' and 'the immortal part, the understanding spirit'. Throughout the play, clothing for the body symbolises the layers of belief or assumption about human goodness which are stripped from the understandings of the chief characters at their moments of tragic insight: 'Off, off you lendings.' But this vision of 'unaccommodated man' is itself distorted. Lear thinking of the 'poore naked wretches', and the blinded Gloucester seeking a covering for Poor Tom, both begin that restoration of man to his 'essential vesture of creation', to a faith in his own humanity, which is completed when Cordelia wakens the newly-dressed Lear and when Edgar reveals himself to the father he has saved from despair. The theme of dress and disguise is used as effectively, but with quite different import, in *Measure for Measure*. It produces a telling play on words in the speech in which Isabella reveals Angelo's villainy to her brother:

> Oh 'tis the cunning *Liuerie* of hell,
> The damnest bodie to inuest, and couer
> In prenzie gardes; dost thou thinke Claudio,
> If I would yeeld him my virginitie
> Thou might'st be freed?   (III.i.93–7)

Here the whole of Isabella's dilemma is conveyed in a single word of multiple and contradictory meanings. *Livery* sends our minds back to Angelo's words in the previous scene with Isabella, when he urged her to show herself a woman 'By putting on the destin'd *Liuerie*'. This meaning of 'token of servitude' thus mingles with the sense of 'disguise' in Isabella's words to Claudio to suggest that Angelo is enslaved to the passion from which he pretends to be exempt; and the lines which follow show that here *livery* is also used to mean 'delivery'; that is, in the legal sense of 'delivery of property into a person's

possession' (*N.E.D.* 5a). Isabella can deliver Claudio from death
by delivering herself into Angelo's possession, but this would
in fact be 'the cunning livery of hell', since it would purchase
damnation for both of them.

The most interesting ironic puns occur when Shakespeare
counters a character's play on words with a quibble of his own.
In such triple wordplay Shakespeare is at his dramatic best,
animating his characters to the point where they seem self-
existent, yet making their every word a facet of his own poetic
vision; in fact, satisfying both those readers who are in search
of 'psychological realism' and those who believe a play should
be 'an extended metaphor'. The best examples of this cannot be
detached from a study of the whole play, but a few examples
may be cited here in ascending order of effectiveness. When
Richard Crookback, saying *'Nolo episcopari'* to the request of
Buckingham and the Citizens that he accept the crown, calls it

> the Golden Yoake of Soueraigntie,
> Which *fondly* you would here impose on me,
> (III.vii.145-6)

he uses *fondly* to mean 'foolishly' and also, since he knows the
strength of Buckingham's devotion, 'affectionately'. We the
audience have, however, been admitted to Richard's secret
thoughts and know how rashly foolish Buckingham is to give
affection to such a man; so Shakespeare himself reverts ironically to the character's ostensible meaning of the word. A
more pointed instance is Falstaff's meditation at the beginning
of Act III, scene iii, of the first part of *Henry IV*: 'Well, Ile
repent, and that suddenly, while I am in some *liking*: I shall be
out of heart shortly, and then I shall have no strength to repent'.
Falstaff is punning on the literal sense of *out of heart*—'in poor
physical condition', by contrast with *in liking* meaning plump—
and on the metaphorical sense of 'dispirited'. But the commoner
meaning of *liking* has already prepared us for the dramatic
irony of the second phrase; Falstaff will shortly be out of the
Prince's heart, and the phrase, like 'Banish plumpe Iacke', is one
of foreboding and presages Falstaff's ultimate dismissal.
Finally, there is a powerfully tragic instance of this triple

wordplay in Othello's 'Put out the *light* and then put out the *light*'. If, as Granville-Barker suggests, Othello is carrying a taper steady in his hand, the words suggest a man both performing a ritual and walking in his sleep. They are in effect a kind of black-magic *tenebrae*, in preparation for the deed that Othello has deceived himself into thinking a sacrificial murder which will purge the honour of his family. Othello himself is become a travesty of the man whose self-possession showed itself in the steady rhythms of his speech before Iago set to work and reduced him to incoherence. His language is now only a parody of such rounded harmonies as 'Keepe vp your bright Swords', because the true magnanimity of the noble Othello was rooted in the love of Desdemona, whom he has rejected and is about to destroy. The light Othello puts out is not Desdemona's spirit which *can* be relumed, and which kindles within this scene in a last attempt to protect Othello—'Oh the more Angell she!' It is the light of his own integrity, which he believes he has renewed, but which is in fact extinguished by the deed that makes him an honourable murderer.

These are all isolated examples of words of which the various meanings are shared between Shakespeare and his characters. It can also happen that such a word is reiterated with the same insistence as a Shakespearean key-image, and with the same object of making explicit the governing idea of the play. In a really great play such as *King Lear* this governing idea is never a thesis to be expounded, but an issue to be explored. A question is asked which can only be resolved mimetically, as we live out its implications with the characters. What is the nature of *Nature*? Is *Kind* kind, the eternal fitness of an ordered creation as Hooker portrayed it, or is it red in tooth and claw? The audience cannot give a pat answer to these questions at the end of the play, but each member of it has grasped something of the nature of Nature by exploring every meaning of the word in the company of Lear and Cordelia. In other plays such as *All's Well* and *Timon of Athens*, Shakespeare has a thesis, and this perhaps brings them closer to being morality plays than true dramas; although it is noticeable that in each there is an almost personal note of doubt and protest—Hellena's avowal of unrequited love, Timon's great invective against man's ingratitude—which does not conform to the play's morality dimensions. In each, play upon a single word is among the means used by Shakespeare to clarify the play's leading idea. In the opening scene of *Timon of Athens*, the Poet's allegory of Fortune is a kind of dumbshow to the whole drama, and fixes *fortune* in our mind as the key word. Three meanings of *fortune*: wealth, ill or good hap, and the fickle goddess whose caprices cause the reversal of man's lot, are used interchangeably to hold up the simple and strong theme that those who have large fortunes are seldom fortunate. When Timon says to his friends:

> Pray sit, more welcome are ye to my *Fortunes*,
> Then my *Fortunes* to me, (I.ii.19-20)

the words ironically prepare us for his own immoderate reception of ill fortune, and for the way he will welcome his hollow friends to share that ill fortune at his next banquet. For when Timon grows poor, the 'familiars to his buried *Fortune*' slink away, and there is not left

> One friend to take his *Fortune* by the arme
> And go along with him. (IV.ii.7-8)

In *All's Well* the play is upon *virtue*. In Shakespeare's time the word's commonest meaning of 'moral excellence' was being encroached upon by the meanings of the Italian *virtù*, themselves complex since they implied the social ideal of a whole civilisation. When Bacon wrote: 'Those that are first raised to nobility are commonly more virtuous, but less innocent, than their descendants', he was using the word in its Italianate sense to mean having ability, distinction, brilliance, strength of personality. Other meanings current in Shakespeare's day—masculine courage, feminine chastity, and a divine operative influence—are all explored as Bertram comes to understand the true nature of virtue. Although Hellena is virtuous in the sense of being both chaste and accomplished, Bertram at first refuses her because she is not of noble birth. She may be good in herself, but is not well descended. But Shakespeare sets the wheel of values turning to demonstrate that Hellena's virtue is in fact hers by descent and that Bertram's is inadequate because it is self-made and rootless. Of Hellena we are told: 'Her dispositions shee inherits, which makes faire gifts fairer: for where an vncleane mind carries *vertuous* qualities, there commendations go with pitty, they are *vertues* and traitors too'. (I.i.47-51). That is, her accomplishments are worth little without the moral goodness which is in part inherited and in part a *virtue* or influence of Heaven. Hellena is herself insistent that her skill in healing is a divine gift, the 'help of heaven' and not 'the act of men', so that she can cure the King only by 'the great'st grace lending grace'. This notion of *virtue* as a heavenly influence was strengthened by the Elizabethan theory that plants received their medicinal virtues from the stars, and starry influences are an important *motif* in the language of the play. The divinely-appointed King has also his influence over the lives of his subjects. We are told at the beginning that he 'holds his *virtue*' to Bertram; and by conferring nobility upon Hellena, he is able to give a name to the virtue Heaven has already allowed her:

> If she bee
> All that is *vertuous* (saue what thou dislik'st)
> A poore Phisitians daughter, thou dislik'st
> Of *virtue* for the name. (II.iii.128-231)

Perversely, Bertram refuses to accept Hellena, who is highly descended because she derives her virtue from Heaven, and goes off to cultivate his own *virtù* in the Florentine war. Despite his own military prowess, he is not able to distinguish a real from a specious military *virtù*, and is deceived by the bravado of Parolles until the braggart is unmasked by Bertram's friends: 'It were fit you knew him, least reposing too farre in his *vertue* which he hath not, he might at some great and trustie businesse, in a maine daunger, fayle you' (III.vi.13-16). A similar unmasking of Bertram himself follows, for his *virtù* in war does not render him truly virtuous. 'His sword can neuer winne the honor that he looses'. In his treatment of Hellena, he degenerates from his stock, from the example of his father whose humility 'Might be a copie to these yonger times'. Bertram's discovery that the woman he took for Diana was in fact Hellena symbolises his discovery that, in a sense, he has been right all along. Virtue *is* delegated, descent does matter; the inherent virtue he has pursued turns out to be an illusion, and Hellena's virtue, derived from her ancestry and from Heaven, is the substance:

> *Hel.*　'Tis but the shadow of a wife you see,
> 　　　The name, and not the thing.
> *Ber.*　Both, both, O pardon.　(V.iii.312-13)

Finally, there are certain words whose rich multiplicity of meanings make them, in Johnson's phrase, Shakespeare's favourite playthings, so that they recur from play to play. They are, as it were, brilliant colours individual to Shakespeare's palette, so that a single touch supplied by one of them renders a passage indubitably Shakespearean. Although Shakespeare's puns are too dependent on the reader's fickle responsiveness to be counted and catalogued, a list of his most played-upon words may tell us something further about the functions of the Shakespearean quibble. *Dear* heads the list. Then come *grace*; *will*; *light*; *lie*; *crown*; *hart-heart* and *son-sun*; *colour* and *use*; *shape*; next, are *bear*, *blood*, *die* and *state*; *bond*, *kind*, *prick*, *suit*; *arms*, *bound*, *great*, *high*, *measure*, *natural* and *note*; and lastly, *habit*, *jack*, *mean*, *mortal*, *stomach* and *virtue*.[1]

Some of these words offered irresistible comic puns to Shakespeare. Adam was a gentleman because 'A was the first that euer bore *armes*'; Benedick is 'a very valiant Trencher-man, hee hath an excellent *stomacke*'. Others, like *hart-heart* and *son-sun*, were part of the Elizabethan poet's stock-in-trade. There are others which attracted Shakespeare because their great semantic range enabled them to be 'placed' in every part of the court in brisk rallies of wit. *Jack*, *bear*, and *lie* are such words; and at least ten meanings of *light* are brought into play in the wit-combats of *Love's Labour's Lost*. Moreover the word's range of meaning, between levity and sparkle on the one hand

---

[1] In this list I have not differentiated parts of speech (as *note*, noun, and *note*, verb), because Shakespeare frequently puns on two or more grammatical functions of the same word.

and intellect or even sagacity on the other, is expressive of a dramatic contrast or conflict,[1] and this function is fulfilled by several other words on our list. *Measure* is so employed, as we have seen, in *The Merchant of Venice*. There is a potentially dramatic contrast, too, in the word *use*, which as a noun can mean 'wear and tear' and so 'deterioration' or, at the other extreme, 'investment' and so 'profit, advantage'; and which as a verb can range between the meaning of 'to wear away' and that of 'to employ, especially to employ money by lending it at interest'. There is tension between these two meanings in Sonnet 4:

> Then beautious nigard why doost thou abuse,
> The bountious largesse giuen thee to giue?
> Profitles vserer why doost thou *vse*
> So great a summe of summes yet can'st not liue?

The Sonnets, as well as the plays, make effective use of the contrast of meaning in another ambivalent word, *will*. In the sense of 'volition' or 'resolution', it can imply something as certain of being put into effect as a last will and testament. But it can also imply inconstant wilfulness; and in the sense of 'desire' it is the passion which Elizabethan psychology held to be least amenable to the Will.

Some of these words are ambivalent in a particular way. Their range of meanings corresponds to an alteration or expansion of our values during the course of the play's dramatic experience. Words such as *great, high, blood, state* and *grace* have restricted meanings of social approbation, but Shakespeare undermines their social prestige by recalling for us either their generalised meanings or other restricted senses which supply a critical overtone. *Blood*, for example, often stands for high birth and parentage (*N.E.D.* III), but the King, in *All's Well*, reminds us that it is the common property of human life:

> strange is it that our *bloods*
> Of colour, waight, and heat, pour'd all together,
> Would quite confound distinction: yet stands off
> In differences so mightie.   (II.iii.125-8)

---

[1] See below, pp. 175-6.

When Don John, in *Much Ado*, says 'It better fits my *bloud* to be disdain'd of all, then to fashion a carriage to rob loue from any', he means *blood* in the sense of high birth; but because his bearing is so unlike that of the play's other courtly characters we, with Shakespeare, take *blood* in the sense of 'disposition'. Don John need no motive, the humours of his blood prompt his villainy. Another wide sense of the word, which Shakespeare contrasts with the restricted social one, is that of 'lust':

> *Blood*, thou art *blood*,
> Let's write good Angell on the Deuills horne
> 'Tis not the Deuills Crest.
> (*Measure for Measure*, II.iv.15-16)

That is, neither high birth nor his seemingly phlegmatic temper of mind exempts Angelo from common human appetite. The richest of all uses of the word is in Othello's terrifying cry: 'Oh blood, blood, blood' (III.iii.452), which is at once an oath, a threat of violence, an accusation of Desdemona and, in its echo of 'My blood begins my safer guides to rule', an indication that Othello's self-command will break under the strain of a passion he has himself feared to acknowledge, but which Iago has always perfectly understood.

Other words are made ambivalent by the opposition of a quite indifferent, unemotive sense and a strongly emotive meaning. *Virtue*, *kind* and *natural* have already been touched upon. *Dear* is equally powerful; the whole story of Coleridge's marriage lies in the sentence: 'Dear Sara accidentally emptied a skillin of boiling milk on my foot.' Out of all the various senses of the word, Shakespeare most likes to play on the unemotive meaning of 'costly, expensive' and the emotive meaning of 'cherished'. The effect of this varies from the matter-of-factness with which Portia masks her love for Bassanio—'Since you are *deere* bought, I will loue you *deere*'—and the cynicism of Sir Toby—'I haue beene *deere* to him lad, some two thousand strong or so'—to the bitter irony of Gaunt's lament over his farmed-out country—'this *deere-deere* Land', of Leontes' repudiation of his queen—'Let what is *deare* in Sicily, be cheape', and of Shakespeare himself in the Sonnets—'Thou best of *deerest*, and mine onely care'.

There remains one small group from these favourite Shakespearean puns which are perhaps the most characteristic of all.
Nearly every play in the canon is concerned with some aspect
of revelation or discovery. A character, and we with him, finds
truth beneath the appearance of things, both in his own nature
('Who is it that can tell me who I am?') and in outward cir-
cumstance. Shakespeare's wordplay contributes much to this
theme of appearance and reality, as we can see by looking at all
the instances of a word like *habit*. A habit is something that is
so much part of our normal behaviour that it is second nature
with us; but the word can carry a strongly contrasting meaning
in the sense of 'dress' and, more particularly, the religious dress
which can be the garb of hypocrisy. *Suit* and *colour* belong to
this group of words; so do the rather less frequent *countenance*,
character and *face*. Once we have grasped the special Elizabethan
meaning of *shape*, 'a disguise or masking costume' in such
contexts as Prospero's words to Ariel: 'Goe take this *shape*',
the interplay becomes dramatically alive between this sense
and the more usual one of 'essential form' (as an egg is known
by its shape). When Richard Crookback asks Elizabeth for
help in wooing her daughter, she replies that he had best tell
her daughter how he has butchered her kindred:

> There is no other way,
> Vnlesse thou could'st put on some other *shape*,
> And not be Richard, that hath done all this.
> > (*Richard III*, IV.iv.286-8)

Richard's misshapen body is to her the inevitable sign of his
deformity of character; but before the scene ends, Richard's
shape, or disguise of the protesting lover, has deceived Elizabeth
into carrying out his wishes. As Hamlet remarks, the devil has
power to assume a pleasing shape; and inevitably the word
reverberates through *Hamlet*, a play that has so much to do
with the unmasking of villainy. In this as in other so-called
Problem Plays, the discovery is always of a bad reality beneath
the fair appearance of things. In the other major tragedies, the
discovery is a double one. Fair may be foul, but foul is also fair.
Regan and Goneril are found to be 'naught', but Cordelia, who
seemed nothing, becomes everything to her father. Edgar hides

his loyalty in many shapes, although we soon find the falsehood in Edmund's claim:

> My minde as generous, and my *shape* as true,
> As honest Madams issue.

> (I.ii.8-9)

This double theme of the evil in seeming goodness and the good in seeming evil gives rise to a double irony in the words that Lear speaks when Goneril first shows her true nature:

>   Thou shalt finde,
> That Ile resume the *shape* which thou dost thinke
> I haue cast off for euer.

> (I.iv.332-4)

In so far as Lear's *shape* is the mere trappings of regal authority, the irony of this is negative. Lear, allowed no more than nature needs, himself strips off humanity's robes of office to discover the poor, bare, forked animal beneath them. But the other meaning of *shape*—'essential form'—conveys here a positive promise, to be fulfilled in the fourth Act, that after all his sufferings Lear will recover his dignity as a human being.

A poet makes his discovery of poetic truth only through an exploration of the meanings of words. Because of this, the study of Shakespeare's wordplay can take us to the central experience of each play as surely as can our interest in its imagery, its way of re-telling an old tale, and its explicit statements. The plays which are the theme of the following chapters are not necessarily those which are most rich in wordplay, but they are ones in which the wordplay appears to me to offer a valuable means of access to the heart of the drama.

II

ROMEO AND JULIET

1

Romeo and Juliet is one of Shakespeare's most punning plays; even a really conservative count yields a hundred and seventy-five quibbles. Critics who find this levity unseemly excuse it by murmuring, with the Bad Quarto Capulet, that 'youth's a jolly thing' even in a tragedy. Yet Shakespeare was over thirty, with a good deal of dramatic writing already to his credit, when *Romeo and Juliet* was first performed. He knew what he was about in his wordplay, which is as functional here as in any of his later tragedies. It holds together the play's imagery in a rich pattern and gives an outlet to the tumultuous feelings of the central characters. By its proleptic second and third meanings it serves to sharpen the play's dramatic irony. Above all, it clarifies the conflict of incompatible truths and helps to establish their final equipoise.

Shakespeare's sonnet-prologue offers us a tale of star-crossed lovers and 'The *fearfull passage* of their *death-markt* loue'.[1] *Death-marked* can mean 'marked out for (or by) death; foredoomed'. If, however, we take *passage* in the sense of a voyage (and this sub-meaning prompts *trafficque* in the twelfth line) as well as a course of events, *death-marked* recalls the 'euer fixed marke' of Sonnet 116 and the sea-mark of Othello's utmost sail, and suggests the meaning 'With death as their objective'. The two meanings of *fearful* increase the line's oscillation; the meaning 'frightened' makes the lovers helpless, but they are not necessarily so if the word means 'fearsome' and so suggests that we, the audience, are awe-struck by their undertaking.

---

[1] L.9. The prologue is not given in the Folio, but is found in the second, third and fourth Quartos. My quotations in this chapter are all from the Shakespeare Association facsimile of the Second Quarto.

These ambiguities pose the play's fundamental question at the outset: is its ending frustration or fulfilment? Does Death choose the lovers or do they elect to die? This question emerges from the language of the play itself and thus differs from the conventional, superimposed problem: is *Romeo and Juliet* a tragedy of Character or of Fate? which can be answered only by a neglect or distortion of the play as a dramatic experience. To blame or excuse the lovers' impetuosity and the connivance of others is to return to Arthur Broke's disapproval of unhonest desire, stolen contracts, drunken gossips and auricular confession. Recent critics have, I believe, come nearer to defining the play's experience when they have stressed the *Liebestod* of the ending and suggested that the love of Romeo and Juliet is the tragic passion that seeks its own destruction. Certainly nearly all the elements of the *amour-passion* myth as it has been defined by Denis de Rougemont[1] are present in the play. The love of Romeo and Juliet is immediate, violent and final. In the voyage imagery of the play[2] they abandon themselves to a rudderless course that must end in shipwreck:

> Thou desperate Pilot, now at once run on
> The dashing Rocks, thy seasick weary barke:
> Heeres to my Loue. (V.iii.117-19)

The obstacle which is a feature of the *amour-passion* legend is partly external, the family feud; but it is partly a sword of the lovers' own tempering since, unlike earlier tellers of the story, Shakespeare leaves us with no explanation of why Romeo did not put Juliet on his horse and make for Mantua. A *leitmotiv* of the play is Death as Juliet's bridegroom; it first appears when Juliet sends to find Romeo's name: 'if he be married, My graue is like to be my wedding bed'. At the news of Romeo's banishment Juliet cries 'And death not Romeo, take my maiden head', and she begs her mother, rather than compel her to marry Paris, to 'make the Bridall bed In that dim Monument where Tibalt lies'. The theme grows too persistent to be mere dramatic irony:

---

[1] *L'Amour et l'Occident* (Paris 1939).
[2] See Kenneth Muir and Sean O'Loughlin, *The Voyage to Illyria* (1937), p. 72.

> O sonne, the night before thy wedding day
> Hath death laine with thy wife, there she lies,
> Flower as she was, deflowred by him,
> Death is my sonne in law, death is my heire.
> My daughter he hath wedded.   (IV.v.35-9)

Romeo, gazing at the supposedly dead Juliet, could well believe

> that vnsubstantiall death is amorous,
> And that the leane abhorred monster keepes
> Thee here in darke to be his parramour.
> (V.iii.103-5)

Most significant of all, there is Juliet's final cry:

> O *happy* dagger
> This is thy sheath, there rust and let me *dye*.
> (V.iii.169-70)

where *happy* implies not only 'fortunate to me in being ready to my hand' but also 'successful, fortunate in itself' and so suggests a further quibble on *die*. Death has long been Romeo's rival and enjoys Juliet at the last.

In all these aspects *Romeo and Juliet* appears the classic literary statement of the *Liebestod* myth in which (we are told) we seek the satisfaction of our forbidden desires; forbidden, according to Freud, because *amour-passion* is inimical to the Race, according to de Rougemont because it is contrary to the Faith. Shakespeare's story conflicts, however, with the traditional myth at several points. Tragic love is always adulterous. Romeo and Juliet marry, and Juliet's agony of mind at the prospect of being married to Paris is in part a concern for her marriage vow: 'My husband is on earth, my faith in heauen'. Again, Romeo faces capture and death, Juliet the horror of being entombed alive, not because they want to die but because they want to live together. These woes are to serve them for sweet discourses in their time to come. In contrast to this, the wish-fulfilment of the *Liebestod* is accomplished only by the story of a suicide pact. Drama has furnished many such plots since the middle of the last century. Deirdre and her lover deliberately return to Ireland and the wrath of Conchubar because it is 'a better thing to be following on to a near death, than to be bending the head down, and dragging with the feet, and seeing one day a blight showing upon love where it is sweet and tender'. What makes Synge's play a tragedy is that the blight does show before the lovers are killed. By itself, the suicide pact offers the audience wish-fulfilment and not *katharsis*. The good cry we enjoy over the worn reels of *Meyerling* bears only a remote relationship to the tragic experience of *Romeo and Juliet*.

The real objection to reading *Romeo and Juliet* as the *Liebestod* myth in dramatic form is that it is anachronistic to align the play with pure myths like that of Orpheus and Eurydice or with the modern restatement of such myths by Anouilh and Cocteau. Shakespeare's intention in writing the play was not that of the post-Freud playwright who finds in a high tale of love and death the objective correlative to his own emotions and those of his audience. We may guess that the story afforded Shakespeare an excited pleasure of recognition because it made explicit a psychological experience; but he did not, on the strength of that recognition, decide to write a play about the death wish. Like Girolamo de la Corte, whose *History of Venise* appeared about the time *Romeo and Juliet* was first acted, Shakespeare believed his lovers to be historical people. He read and retold their adventures with the detached judgment we accord history as well as with the implicated excitement we feel for myth. The story is both near and remote; it goes on all the time in ourselves, but its events belong also to distant Verona in the dog days when the mad blood is stirred to passion and violence. The resultant friction between history and myth, between the story and the fable, kindles the play into great drama. When we explore the language of *Romeo and Juliet* we find that both its wordplay and its imagery abound in those concepts of love as a war, a religion, a malady, which de Rougemont has suggested as the essence of *amour-passion*. If the play were pure myth, the fictionalising of a psychological event, all these elements would combine in a single statement of our desire for a tragic love. But because the play is also an exciting story about people whose objective existence we accept during the two hours' traffic of the stage, these images and quibbles are dramatically 'placed'; to ascertain Shakespeare's intentions in using them we need to see which characters are made to speak them and how they are distributed over the course of the action.

2

Act I begins with some heavy-witted punning from Sampson and Gregory—a kind of verbal tuning-up which quickens our ear for the great music to come. The jests soon broaden. This is one of Shakespeare's most bawdy plays, but the bawdy has always a dramatic function. Here its purpose is to make explicit, at the beginning of this love tragedy, one possible relationship between man and woman: a brutal male dominance expressed in sadistic quibbles. After the brawl has been quelled, the mood of the scene alters 'like a change from wood wind, brass and tympani to an andante on the strings'[1] in Benvolio's tale of Romeo's melancholia; and Romeo himself appears and expresses, in the numbers that Petrarch flowed in, the contrary relationship of the sexes: man's courtly subjection to women's tyranny. Rosaline is a saint, and by his quibbles upon theological terms Romeo shows himself a devotee of the Religion of Love:

> She is too faire, too wise, wisely too faire,
> To merit blisse by making me *dispaire*. (227-8)

Love is a sickness as well as a cult, and Romeo twists Benvolio's request to tell in sadness (that is, seriously) whom he loves, to an expression of *amour-maladie*:

> A sicke man in *sadnesse* makes his will:
> A word ill vrgd to one that is so ill. (208-9)

It is characteristic of this love learnt by rote from the sonnet writers that Romeo should combine images and puns which suggest this slave-like devotion to his mistress with others that imply a masterful attack on her chastity.[2] Love is a man of war in such phrases as 'th' incounter of assailing eies' which, added to the aggressive wordplay of Sampson and Gregory and to the

---

[1] Harley Granville-Barker, *Prefaces to Shakespeare, Second Series* (1930), p. 6.
[2] See G. E. Matthews, 'Sex and the Sonnet', *Essays in Criticism* II (1952), pp. 119-37.

60

paradox of 'ô brawling loue, ô louing hate', reinforce the theme
of ambivalence, the *odi-et-amo* duality of passion.

All the Petrarchan and anti-Petrarchan conventions are thus
presented to us in this first scene: love as malady, as worship,
as war, as conquest. They are presented, however, with an
exaggeration that suggests Romeo is already aware of his own
absurdity and is 'posing at posing'. 'Where shall we dine?' is
a most unlover-like question which gives the show away;
and Benvolio's use of 'in sadnesse' implies that he knows
Romeo's infatuation to be nine parts show. Romeo is in fact
ready to be weaned from Rosaline, and the scene ends with a
proleptic pun that threatens the overthrow of this textbook
language of love. 'Examine other bewties' Benvolio urges, but
for Romeo, 'Tis the way to call hers (exquisit) in question
more'. By *question* he means, with a play upon the etymology
of *exquisite*, 'consideration and conversation'; but we guess, if
we do not know, that Rosaline's charms will be called into
question in another sense when set beside the beauty of Juliet.

Love in Verona may be a cult, a quest or a madness. Marriage
is a business arrangement. Old Capulet's insistence to Paris, in
the next scene, that Juliet must make her own choice, is belied
by later events. Juliet is an heiress, and her father does not
intend to enrich any but a husband of his own choosing:

> *Earth* hath swallowed all my hopes but she,
> Shees the hopefull Lady of my *earth*.   (I.ii.14–15)

This quibbling distinction between *earth* as the grave and
earth as lands (as Steevens points out, *fille de terre* means an
heiress) is confounded when Juliet's hopes of happiness end in
the Capulets' tomb. We recall the dramatic irony of this pun
when Old Capulet speaks his last, moving quibble:

> O brother Mountague, giue me thy hand,
> This is my daughters *ioynture*, for no more
> Can I demaund.   (V.iii.296–8)

The ball scene at Capulet's house is prologued by a revealing
punning-match between Romeo and Mercutio. Romeo's lumber-
ing puns are the wordplay of courtly love: the other masquers
have nimble soles, he has a soul of lead: he is too bound to

earth to bound, too sore from Cupid's darts to soar in the dance. Mercutio's levity, on the other hand, is heightened by his bawdy quibbles. Mercutio appears in early versions of the tale as what is significantly known as a ladykiller, and his dramatic purpose at this moment of the play is to oppose a cynical and aggressive idea of sex to Romeo's love-idolatry and so sharpen the contrast already made in the opening scene. Yet just as Romeo's touch of self-parody then showed him to be ready for a more adult love, so Mercutio's Queen Mab speech implies that his cynicism does not express the whole of his temperament. The falsity of both cynicism and idolatry, already felt to be inadequate by those who hold these concepts, is to be exposed by the love between Romeo and Juliet. Like Chaucer two centuries previously, Shakespeare weighed the ideas of the masterful man and the tyrannical mistress and wisely concluded that 'Love wol nat be constreyned by maistrie'.

For the ball scene, Shakespeare deploys his resources of stagecraft and poetry in a passage of brilliant dramatic counterpoint. Our attention is divided, during the dance, between the reminiscences of the two old Capulets (sketches for Silence and Shallow) and the rapt figure of Romeo who is watching Juliet. Nothing is lost by this, since the talk of the two pantaloons is mere inanity. We are only aware that it has to do with the passage of years too uneventful to be numbered, so that twenty-five is confused with thirty; simultaneously we share with Romeo a timeless minute that cannot be reckoned by the clock. Yet the old men's presence is a threat as well as a dramatic contrast. They have masqued and loved in their day, but ''tis gone, 'tis gone, 'tis gone'.

Romeo's first appraisal of Juliet's beauty is rich not only in its unforgettable images but also in the subtlety of its wordplay. Hers is a 'Bewtie too rich for vse, for earth too deare'. When we recall that *use* means 'employment', 'interest' and 'wear and tear' that *earth* means both 'mortal life' and 'the grave', that *dear* can be either 'cherished' or 'costly' and that there is possibly a play upon *beauty* and *booty* (as there is in *Henry IV* part 1, I.ii.28), the line's range of meanings becomes very wide indeed. Over and above the contrast between her family's valuation of her as sound stock in the marriage market and Romeo's estimate that she is beyond all price, the words contain a self-contradictory dramatic irony. Juliet's beauty is too rich for use in the sense that it will be laid in the tomb after a brief enjoyment; but for that very reason it will never be faded and worn. And if she is *not* too dear for earth since Romeo's love is powerless to keep her out of the tomb, it is true that she is too rare a creature for mortal life. Not all these meanings are consciously present to the audience, but beneath the conscious level they connect with later images and quibbles and are thus brought into play before the tragedy is over.

The counterpoint of the scene is sustained as Romeo moves towards his new love against the discordant hate and rage of her cousin. Tybalt rushes from the room, threatening to convert seeming sweet to bitter gall, at the moment Romeo touches Juliet's hand. The lovers meet and salute each other in a sonnet full of conceits and quibbles on the Religion of Love—'palme to palme is holy Palmers kis'; 'grant thou least faith turne to dispaire'; 'Saints do not moue'—for the place is public and they must disguise their feelings beneath a social persiflage. The real strength of those feelings erupts in Romeo's pun—'O *deare* account!'—and in Juliet's paradox—'My onely loue sprung from my onely hate'—when each learns the other's identity, and the elements of youth and experience, love and hate, which have been kept apart throughout the scene, are abruptly juxtaposed. Then the torches are extinguished and the scene ends with a phrase of exquisite irony, when the Nurse speaks to Juliet as to a tired child after a party: 'Come lets away, the strangers all are gone.' Romeo is no longer a stranger and Juliet no longer a child.

A quibbling sonnet on love between enemies and some of Mercutio's ribald jests separate this scene from that in Capulet's orchard.[1] It is as if we must be reminded of the social and

---

[1] Mercutio's 'This field-bed is too cold for me to sleepe' seems to be an echo of the Nurse's words to the lovers in Broke's poem:
> Loe here a fielde, (she shewd a fieldbed ready dight)
> Where you may, if you list, in armes, revenge your selfe by fight.
As often with Shakespeare, a piece of rhetorical decoration in the source has become an integral part of the play's imagery, by prompting its quibbles on love as war.

sexual strife before we hear Romeo and Juliet declare the perfect harmony of their feelings for each other. At first Romeo seems still to speak the language of idolatry, but the 'winged messenger of heauen' belongs to a different order of imagination from the faded conceits of his devotion to Rosaline. The worn commonplaces of courtship are swept aside by Juliet's frankness. One of the few quibbles in the scene is on *frank* in the meanings of 'generous' and 'candid, open', and it introduces Juliet's boldest and most beautiful avowal of her feelings:

> *Rom.* O wilt thou leaue me so vnsatisfied?
> *Iul.* What satisfaction canst thou haue to night?
> *Rom.* Th'exchange of thy loues faithful vow for mine.
> *Iul.* I gaue thee mine before thou didst request it:
> And yet I would it were to giue againe.
> *Rom.* Woldst thou withdraw it, for what purpose loue?
> *Iul.* But to be franke and giue it thee againe,
> And yet I wish but for the thing I haue,
> My bountie is as boundlesse as the sea,
> My loue as deepe, the more I giue to thee
> The more I haue, for both are infinite. (II.ii.125-35)

Thus the distribution of wordplay upon the concepts of love-war, love-idolatry, love-sickness, serves to show that the feelings of Romeo and Juliet for each other are something quite different from the *amour-passion* in which de Rougemont finds all these disorders. For Romeo doting upon Rosaline, love was a malady and a religion; for Mercutio it is sheer lunacy ('a great naturall that runs lolling vp and downe') or a brutal conquest with no quarter given. All these notions are incomplete and immature compared to the reality. When Romeo meets Mercutio the next morning a second quibbling-match ensues in which the bawdy expressive of love-war and love-madness is all Mercutio's. Romeo's puns, if silly, are gay and spontaneous in comparison with his laboured conceits on the previous evening. Then, as he explained to Benvolio, he was not himself, not Romeo. Now Mercutio cries: 'now art thou sociable, now art thou Romeo'. In fact Romeo and Juliet have experienced a self-discovery. Like Donne's happy lovers, they 'possess one world, each hath one and is one'; a world poles apart from the Nirvana quested by romantic love. The play is a tragedy, not because the love of Romeo for Juliet is in its nature tragic, but because the ending achieves the equilibrium of great tragedy. The final victory of time and society over the lovers is counterpoised by the knowledge that it is, in a sense, *their* victory; a victory not only over time and society which would have made them old and worldly in the end (whereas their deaths heal the social wound), but over the most insidious enemy of love, the inner hostility that 'builds a Hell in Heaven's despite' and which threatens in the broad jests of Mercutio. For we believe in the uniqueness of Romeo's and Juliet's experience at the same time as we know it to be, like other sublunary things, neither perfect nor permanent. If our distress and satisfaction are caught up in the fine balance of great tragedy at the end of the play, it is because, throughout, the wordplay and imagery, the conduct of the action and the grouping of characters contribute to that balance. The lovers' confidence is both heightened and menaced by a worldly wisdom, cynicism and resignation which, for the reason that candle-holders see more of the game, we are not able to repudiate as easily as they can do.

3

The play's central paradox of love's strength and fragility is most clearly expressed in the short marriage scene (II.vi). On the one hand there is Romeo's triumphant boast:

> come what sorrow can,
> It cannot counteruaile the exchange of ioy
> That one short minute giues me in her sight:
> Do thou but close our hands with holy words,
> Then loue deuouring death do what he dare,
> It is inough I may but call her mine.   (3-8)

On the other hand there are the forebodings of Friar Laurence:

> These violent delights haue violent endes,
> And in their triumph die like fier and powder:
> Which as they kisse *consume*,   (9-11)

where *consume* means both 'reach a consummation' (*N.E.D.* v.[2]) and 'burn away, be destroyed'. These conflicting themes of satisfaction and frustration coalesce in the Friar's words on Juliet's entry:

> Here comes the Lady, Oh so *light* a foote
> Will *nere weare out* the euerlasting flint.   (16-17)

An ambiguity of pronunciation between 'near' and 'ne'er' and another of meaning in *wear out*[1] enable us to distinguish four possible readings here before, with cormorant delight, we swallow the lot. Juliet's foot is so light that

- (i) it will never wear away the everlasting flint;
- (ii) it will never last it out;
- (iii) it will nearly outlast it;
- (iv) it will nearly wear it away.

The first of these is the obvious meaning, platitudinously suited to the speaker. The second anticipates our fear that the lovers are too beset with enemies on the hard road of life to be able to last the course, whereas the third contradicts this by saying that Juliet's love and beauty, because time will not have the chance to wear them away, will last in their fame nearly as long as the rocks of earth. And this contradiction is heightened by (iv) in which *light* has a suggestion of Juliet's luminous beauty,[2] and the flint is that of a flintlock; so that the line is connected with the sequence of paradoxical light images running through the play. Love is spoken of as a sudden spark or a flash of lightning. Juliet's forebodings in the balcony scene—

> I haue no ioy of this contract to night,
> It is too rash, too vnaduisd, too sudden,
> Too like the lightning which doth cease to bee,
> Ere one can say, it lightens   (II.ii.117-20)

—are deepened here by the Friar's talk of fire and powder and again in the next act by his reproaches to Romeo:

---

[1] As in the shoe polish advertisement: 'They're well-worn but they've worn well.' For discussion of the *Romeo and Juliet* passage see the correspondence in the *T.L.S.* for April 3, 17 and 24 and May 1, 1943.

[2] There are previous puns on *light*:

Away from light steales home my heauie sonne (I.i.142); Being but heauie I will beare the light (I.iv.12); And not impute this yeelding to light loue, Which the darke night hath so discouered (II.ii.105-6).

> Thy wit, that ornament, to shape and loue,
> Mishapen in the conduct of them both:
> Like powder in a skillesse souldiers flaske,
> Is set a fier by thine owne ignorance.   (III.iii.129-32)

In sum, love is as easily extinguishable as it appears to Lysander in *A Midsummer Night's Dream*:

> Briefe as the lightning in the collied night,
> That (in a spleene) vnfolds both heauen and earth;
> And ere a man hath power to say, behold,
> The iawes of darknesse do deuoure it vp:
> So quicke bright things come to confusion.   (I.i.145-9)

Yet Romeo, when he experiences 'a *lightning* before death', uses the pun not only to imply that he has enjoyed a lightning brief happiness before being

> dischargd of breath,
> As violently, as hastie powder fierd
> Doth hurry from the fatall Canons wombe,
>
> (V.i.63-5)

but also to sustain the image of Juliet's luminous beauty which makes 'This Vault a feasting presence full of light'. For alongside the images of sparks, torches, lightning, are others which associate Romeo and Juliet with the unquenchable heavenly lights. Mercutio's 'We waste our lights in vaine, light lights by day' is ironically apposite to Romeo's love of Rosaline, who is a mere candle before the sun that breaks from Juliet's window. Two passages which have been slighted as conceits are an essential part of this theme:

> Two of the fairest starres in all the heauen,
> Hauing some busines do[1] entreate her eyes,
> To twinckle in their spheres till they returne.
> What if her eyes were there, they in her head,
> The brightnesse of her cheek wold shame those stars,
> As day-light doth a lampe, her eye in heauen,
> Would through the ayrie region streame so bright,
> That birds would sing, and thinke it were not night.
>
> (II.ii.15-22)

---

[1] For the Second Quarto's *to*.

> Giue me my Romeo, and when I shall die,
> Take him and cut him out in little starres,
> And he will make the face of heauen so fine,
> That all the world will be in loue with night,
> And pay no worship to the garish Sun.
>
> (III.ii.21-5)

Romeo and Juliet stellify each other, the love which appears to be quenched as easily as a spark is extinguished is, in fact, made as permanent as the sun and stars when it is set out of the range of time.

The same paradox is sustained by the flower images which are closely associated with those of light. The 'gather the rose' theme was of course inevitable in a love tragedy of the High Renaissance. Shakespeare's rose imagery, however, is more than rhetorical, and serves to stress the central themes of the play.[1] The rose was dramatically appropriate as a love symbol because it was so often a prey to the invisible worm: 'Loathesome canker liues in sweetest bud.' Romeo is devoured by his infatuation for Rosaline 'as is the bud bit with an enuious worme' and the Friar, gathering herbs, moralises over the adulteration of the good in a life by its evil until 'the Canker death eates vp that Plant'. Romeo and Juliet are spared this. Death lies on Juliet just as its earlier semblance had done

> like an vntimely frost,
> Vpon the sweetest flower of all the field.
> (IV.v.28-9)

This early frost forestalls the heat of the sun as well as the blight in the bud, since a further fitness of the image consists in the speed with which both roses and 'fresh female buds'[2] bloom and wither in the south. Although Lady Capulet seems never to have been young she tells Juliet

> I was your mother, much vpon these yeares
> That you are now a maide,   (I.iii.72-3)

[1] As the author of 2 *Henry VI*, Shakespeare must almost unconsciously have connected rose images with the rivalry of two great houses. For the light-flowers cluster see I.i.139-45 and 156-8; I.ii.24-30; II.ii.117-22.

[2] I borrow the phrase from the Bad Quarto. The accepted texts have 'fresh fennell buds'.

and the cruelty of Verona's summer is implicit in Old Capulet's words:

> Let two more Sommers wither in their pride,
> Ere we may thinke her ripe to be a bride.
>
> (I.ii.10–11)

The marriage scene, after its strong statement of love as the victor-victim of time, closes with a quibbling passage already discussed[1] in which Romeo and Juliet defy time's most powerful allies. Romeo, in an image of music, challenges the notion that passion is discordant by nature, Juliet rejects the prudence of social considerations in her declaration of love's richness—'I cannot sum vp sum of halfe my wealth.' This last image is a foretaste of *Antony and Cleopatra*, and it would be interesting to compare the success of love's three enemies in Shakespeare's three double-titled tragedies. In *Troilus and Cressida* they win hands down. Society, in the shape of the Trojan War, again compels secrecy and again separates the lovers; the inner corruption of love itself makes Cressida unfaithful; and the burden of the play is that 'Loue, friendship, charity, are subiects all To enuious and calumniating time'. By contrast, *Antony and Cleopatra* is a clear victory for the lovers. Society, seen as the pomp of Rome, is a world well lost; the dismal drunken party we witness on Pompey's barge contrasts poorly with the revels of Antony and Cleopatra—which are left to our imagination. The lovers are old and wise enough to be reconciled to the ambivalence of their feelings, which is implicit in the play's imagery. Finally, time cannot harm them when they have eternity in their lips and eyes; at the end of the play Cleopatra is again for Cydnus to meet Mark Antony.

In *Romeo and Juliet* love's enemies have a Pyrrhic victory which begins with the slaying of Mercutio at the beginning of Act III. Like many of Shakespeare's characters, Mercutio dies with a quibble that asserts his vitality in the teeth of death. He jests as long as he has breath; only if we ask for him *tomorrow* shall we find him a grave man. But it is a grim joke, to accompany a dying curse. The Elizabethans, who believed in the power of curses, would have seen in the play's subsequent

[1] See above, p. 13

events the working-out of Mercutio's cynical knowledge that love is inseparably commingled with hate in human affairs. Romeo kills Tybalt, the cousin whose name he now tenders as dearly as his own. Juliet responds to the news with an outburst—'O serpent heart hid with a flowring face . . .' which, by recalling the loving hate of Romeo's infatuation with Rosaline, threatens the harmony and permanence of the love between Romeo and Juliet. She recovers her balance, but we have felt the tremor and know that even these lovers cannot sustain many such shocks.

Some of the most notorious puns in Shakespeare occur in this scene between Juliet and her Nurse, when the Nurse's confusion misleads Juliet into thinking Romeo has killed himself:

> Hath Romeo slaine himselfe? say thou but *I*,
> And that bare vowell *I* shall poyson more
> Then the death darting[1] *eye* of Cockatrice,
> *I* am not *I*, if there be such an *I*.
> Or those *eyes* shut[1], that makes thee answere *I*:
> If he be slaine say *I*, or if not, no.
>
> (III.ii.45-50)

Excuses might be made for this. It does achieve a remarkable sound-effect by setting Juliet's high-pitched keening of 'I' against the Nurse's moans of 'O Romeo, Romeo'. It also sustains the eye imagery of Juliet's great speech at the opening of this scene: the runaways' eyes, the blindness of love, Juliet hooded like a hawk, Romeo as the eye of heaven. But excuses are scarcely needed since this is one of Shakespeare's first attempts to reveal a profound disturbance of mind by the use of quibbles.[2] Romeo's puns in the next scene at Friar Laurence's cell are of the same kind: flies may kiss Juliet, but he must fly from her; the Friar, though a friend *professed*, will offer him no sudden mean of death, though ne'er so mean; he longs to know what his concealed lady says to their cancelled love. This is technically crude, and perhaps we do well to omit it in modern productions; but it represents a psychological discovery that Shakespeare was to put to masterly use in later plays. Against

---

[1] For the Second Quarto's *arting* and *shot*.
[2] He had already done so in *Two Gentlemen of Verona* (see above p.32) but the device is less startling in a comedy.

this feverish language of Romeo's, Shakespeare sets the Friar's sober knowledge that lovers have suffered and survived these calamities since the beginning of time. For the Friar, 'the world is broad and wide', for Romeo, 'there is no world without Verona wall'. When the Friar tries to dispute with him of his 'estate', the generalised, prayer-bookish word suggests that Romeo's distress is the common human lot, and we believe as much even while we join with Romeo in his protest: 'Thou canst not speak of that thou dost not feele.' Tragedy continually restates the paradox that 'all cases are unique and very similar to others'.

The lovers' parting at dawn sustains this contradiction. Lovers' hours may be full eternity, but the sun must still rise. Their happiness has placed them out of the reach of fate; but from now on, an accelerating series of misfortunes is to confound their triumph in disaster without making it any less of a triumph. With Lady Capulet's arrival to announce the match with Paris, love's enemies begin to close in. Juliet meets her mother with equivocations which suggest that Romeo's 'snowie Doue' has grown wise as serpents since the story began, and which prepare us for her resolution in feigning death to remain loyal to Romeo:

> Indeed I neuer shall be satisfied
> With Romeo, till I behold him. Dead
> Is my poore heart so for a kinsman vext.[1]
>
> (III.v.94-6)

This is a triple ambiguity, with one meaning for Juliet, another for her mother and a third for us, the audience: Juliet will never in fact see Romeo again until she wakes and finds him dead beside her.

A pun which has escaped most editors is made by Paris at the beginning of Act IV. He tells the Friar he has talked little of love with Juliet because 'Venus smiles not in a house of teares'. Here *house of tears* means, beside the bereaved Capulet household

---

[1] The Arden editor, following Theobald's reading, prints it thus:
  Indeed, I never shall be satisfied
  With Romeo, till I behold him—dead—
  Is my poor heart so for a kinsman vex'd.

an inauspicious section of the heavens—perhaps the eighth house or 'house of death'. Spenser's line 'When oblique Saturne sate in the house of agonyes'[1] shows that the image was familiar to the Elizabethans, and here it adds its weight to the lovers' yoke of inauspicious stars. But this is one of very few quibbles in the last two acts. The wordplay which, in the first part of the play, served to point up the meaning of the action is no longer required. What quibbles there are in the final scenes have, however, extraordinary force. Those spoken by Romeo after he has drunk the poison reaffirm the paradox of the play's experience at its most dramatic moment:

> O *true* Appothecary:
> Thy drugs are *quicke*. Thus with a kisse I die.
> (V.iii.119-20)

Like the Friar's herbs, the apothecary's poison both heals and destroys. He is *true* not only because he has spoken the truth to Romeo in describing the poison's potency, but because he has been true to his calling in finding the salve for Romeo's ills. His drugs are not only speedy, but also *quick* in the sense of 'life-giving'. Romeo and Juliet 'cease to die, by dying'.

It is the prerogative of poetry to give effect and value to incompatible meanings. In *Romeo and Juliet*, several poetic means contribute to this end: the paradox, the recurrent image, the juxtaposition of old and young in such a way that we are both absorbed by and aloof from the lovers' feelings, and the sparkling wordplay. By such means Shakespeare ensures that our final emotion is neither the satisfaction we should feel in the lovers' death if the play were a simple expression of the *Liebestod* theme, nor the dismay of seeing two lives thwarted and destroyed by vicious fates, but a tragic equilibrium which includes and transcends both these feelings.

[1] *The Faerie Queene*, II.ix.52.

III

RICHARD THE SECOND

When Dogberry, briefing his Watch in the third act of *Much Ado*, commands them to 'bid any man stand in the Princes name', he is met by the disconcerting question 'How if a will not stand?' The same problem, in a historic instead of a comic context, confronts the Duke of York at Bolingbroke's return from banishment, and like Dogberry he has to let the invader pass when the magic of the royal name fails to work. The King's power which lies in York's 'loyal bosom' is only verbal authority, not material strength. Shakespeare's plays have many characters who, like Harry Hereford and the watchman of Messina, question the power of words; if the sixteenth century as a whole preserved a medieval faith in verbal magic, it had also its Sancho Panzas who knew that fine words buttered no parsnips, its Hotspurs who could call up spirits from the vasty deep but took leave to doubt if they would come when so called. It was to be expected that Hotspur, a verbal sceptic, would also be a political rebel. For ultimately, in a process that took some two centuries, the question 'What's in a name?' was to destroy Authority. To doubt the real relationship between name and nominee, between a word and the thing it signified, was to shake the whole structure of Elizabethan thought and society.[1]

Richard II is a play about the efficacy of a king's words. Shakespeare here sets 'the word against the word': the words of a poet against the words of a politician. Richard is a poet, but not, of course, for the reason that as a character in a poetic drama he speaks verse which is magnificent in its imagery and cadence. If the whole play were in prose, he would still be a poet by virtue of his faith in words; his loss of this faith and

---

[1] See Chapter VIII below for a fuller discussion of this.

his consequent self-discovery that for all the wordy flattery of others he is not agueproof, constitute Richard's tragedy. Bolingbroke, on the other hand, knows words have no inherent potency of meaning, but by strength of character and force of arms he is able to make them mean what he wants them to mean. The historical, as distinct from the tragic, action of the play lies in Bolingbroke's perilous contravention of the divine decree which made Richard king; and this historical action is not self-contained but belongs to the whole sequence of the mature Histories.

These two themes are supported and often impelled by the play's verbal ambiguities which nearly all have to do with language. The words most often played upon include *breath* in the meaning of 'respiration', 'life', 'time for breathing', 'utterance' and 'will expressed in words';[1] *title* in meanings ranging from 'legal right', through 'appellation of honour' to 'a label'; *name* either as a superficial labelling or as inherent reputation; *honour* in a range of meanings to be further developed when Falstaff answers his own question: 'What is honour? a word!'; *tongue* as the mere organ that makes sounds or as the whole complex organisation of a language; *sentence* meaning 'a unit of speech', 'judgment', 'an apophthegm' or 'significance'; and the word *word* itself, signifying on the one hand 'an element of speech' and on the other, 'contention', 'command', 'promise', 'apophthegm' or 'divine utterance'. The almost polar extremes of meaning in many of these words contribute to the rigid symmetry of the play's action, the descent of Richard and rise of Bolingbroke like buckets in a well. At the same time, the most delicate nuances of meaning between these extremes are used to give a poetic subtlety which can only be suggested here in a brief survey of the play's development.

1

Shakespeare uses his favorite device of a play-within-a-play at the very beginning of *Richard II*. As soon as the playhouse trumpet has sounded and the actors are entered Richard, with his own triple blast of resonant language, stages a miniature

[1] The *N.E.D.* gives an illustration from Burns which is apposite here: 'Princes and lords are but the breath of kings'.

drama between Bolingbroke and Mowbray, which he promises himself shall be a good show:

> Then call them to our presence face to face,
> And frowning brow to brow our selues will heare,
> The accuser and the accused freely speake.[1]
>
> (I.i.15-17)

The poet is never more a maker than when he enacts the very semblance of life in a play; and the poet Richard combines the work of producer and chief actor when he attempts to stage, by royal command, a drama of quarrel and reconciliation in which he himself will play the controlling part of *deus ex machina*. But Bolingbroke and Mowbray, for all the splendour of their rhetoric, are not content with words. They are in such haste to make their accusations good by their deeds, that the words themselves take on the nature of action: Bolingbroke stuffs the name of traitor down Mowbray's throat; Mowbray, as he spits out his counter-challenge, retaliates by cramming these terms of abuse *doubled* down Bolingbroke's. Each detail of Bolingbroke's charge is prefaced by his resolve to verify his words with deeds:

> Looke what I speake, my life shall proue it true . . .
>
> Besides I say, and will in battle proue . . .
>
> Further I say and further will maintaine . . .
>
> (87, 92, 98)

His last accusation, that Mowbray complotted in the murder of the Duke of Gloucester, whose blood

> like sacrificing Abels cries,
> Euen from the tounglesse Cauernes of the earth,
>
> (104-5)

lends ironic support to Bolingbroke's belief that deeds speak louder than words. Shakespeare's audience, whether or not they had seen *Thomas of Woodstock*, would know that Richard was implicated in Gloucester's death and that Richard's own

[1] The quotations from the play in this chapter are from the First Quarto, 1597 (Griggs Facsimile, 1890), except those from the abdication episode in Act IV, for which the Folio text has been used.

murder was a proof of the belief that blood would have blood; but as the instigator of Richard's death, Bolingbroke calls upon himself that curse of Cain which he pronounces against Exton at the end of the play.[1]

The king has no wish to see Mowbray's guilt exposed by a trial of arms, and he attempts to end this scene of quarrel by his own trite epilogue on the theme of 'Forget, forgive'. But neither contestant will swallow his words. Mowbray's 'fair *name*' is more to him than an appellation: it is his reputation, the dearest part of him—'Mine honour is my life, both grow in one.' Bolingbroke will not be *crestfallen*: unless he can prove his words in battle, he has no right to the armorial bearings which signify his nobility. The words of both are pitted against the king's words, and by force of character they carry the day. The king who was 'not borne to sue, but to commaund' must wait until the meeting at Coventry for his decree in Council to carry the authority which his own words lack.

A dancing tattoo of language accompanies the flourishes and fanfares of trumpets at the Coventry lists. There is a gaiety of rhythm and image in the farewell speeches of Mowbray and Bolingbroke; both speak of the approaching fight as a feast, both are savouring this chance to prove by action the truth of their words. But the king asserts the authority of his word in Council, the fight is called off and the champions banished the kingdom. At this point Mowbray, not an important character in the plot, is given a significant speech full of puns upon *breath*, *sentence* and *tongue*—words which shuttle back and forth to weave the elaborate verbal fabric of the play. In contrast to the 'golden vncontrould enfranchisment' promised by the contest, he now faces an enforced inactivity among people whose language he cannot speak. The irony of this becomes clear in the fourth act, when a noisy and abortive war of words between the nobles is silenced by Carlisle's account of how

[1] With Cayne go wander through shades of night,
And neuer shew thy head by day nor light.
Pace Dr Wilson, this framing of the play's action between two occurrences of the same image almost proves these lines to be Shakespeare's. 'By day nor light' is lame, but not 'merely nonsense' (New Cambridge ed, p. lxx), since it could presumably mean 'by real or artificial light'.

Mowbray in fact led a life of honourable action after his banishment:

> Manie a time hath banisht Norffolke fought,
> For Iesu Christ in glorious Christian feild,
> Streaming the ensigne of the Christian Crosse,
> Against black Pagans, Turkes, and Saracens,
> And toild with workes of warre, retird him selfe
> To Italie, and there at Venice gaue
> His bodie to that pleasant Countries earth,
> And his pure soule vnto his Captaine Christ,
> Vnder whose coulours he had fought so long.
>
> (IV.i.92-100)

Placed as they are in the play, these lines strengthen its symmetry of action. As Bolingbroke's star rises, he himself declines in our estimation; as the fortunes of Richard and his friends deteriorate they win new regard and sympathy from the audience. When this praise of Mowbray's 'pure soul' is spoken, Bolingbroke is king, and this gives the words a further ironic value. Throughout his reign Bolingbroke will long to expiate his usurpation in a crusade, but that hope is destroyed when he fulfils a quibbling prophecy by dying in 'Jerusalem'—the Jerusalem Chamber at Westminster.

The first climax of the play is reached at Coventry. The king plays with the power of the royal word by changing the years of Bolingbroke's banishment from ten to six. It is a dramatic instant, the moment when, with Richard at the height of his power and Bolingbroke at the lowest reach of his fortunes, the buckets begin to move; for Bolingbroke seems suddenly to comprehend and covet the efficacy of a king's words:

> How long a time lies in one little *word*,
> Foure lagging winters and foure wanton springes,
> End in a *word*, such is the *breath* of Kinges.
>
> (I.iii.213-15)

By Elizabethan analogy the breath of the king should be a life-giving force, a human imitation of the Divine Spirit; but whereas Bolingbroke's reaction to the king's words is the envious acknowledgment of their god-like power, Gaunt sees only the king's human limitations and speaks of them in words which echo Bolingbroke's, but with subtle differences of meaning:

> Thou canst helpe time to furrow me with age,
> But stoppe no wrinckle in his pilgrimage:
> Thy *word* is currant with him for my death,
> But dead, thy kingdome cannot buy my *breath*.
>
> (229-32)

The court leaves. Gaunt tries to console Bolingbroke with empty words that bear no relation to his real thoughts, while his son cannot find words that are adequate to his grief,

> When the tongues office should be prodigall
> To breathe the aboundant *dolor* of the heart.   (256-7)

The pun is less trivial than it seems; Bolingbroke will be found to be much concerned with the *value* of words, which for him lies only in the actuality of the things they signify. Words for him can never make or obscure facts. When Gaunt bids him call his exile 'a *trauaile* that thou takst for pleasure' and a '*foyle* wherein thou art to set, The pretious Iewell of thy home returne', Bolingbroke takes up *travel* in its harsher sense of 'travail' and *foil* in the meaning 'frustration, obstacle' to fashion the bitter wordplay of his reply:

> Must I not serue a long apprentishood,
> To forreine passages, and in the end,
> Hauing my freedome, boast of nothing else,
> But that I was a *iourneyman* to griefe.   (271-4)

At the end of the scene, the contrast between the outlooks of father and son is formalised into two rhetorical speeches. Gaunt sententiously proclaims that there is no virtue but necessity, and Bolingbroke, who knows the real meaning of Richard's sentence, cries out against such deceptive verbiage:

> Oh who can hold a fier in his hand,
> By thinking on the frosty Caucasus?   (294-5)

This is just what Richard, who has always been deceived by the seeming power of words, will strive to do when his fortunes turn. Bolingbroke, although he is not to be so deceived, uses the conceptual power of words to snare others; and Richard implies this when he describes his cousin's departure after his banishment:

> Our self and Bushie,
> Obserued his *courtship* to the common people,

How he did seeme to diue into their harts,
With humble and familiar *courtesie*,
What *reuerence* he did throw away on slaues,
Wooing poore craftsmen with the *craft* of smiles
And patient *vnder-bearing* of his fortune
As twere to *banish their affects* with him. (I.iv.23-30)

Bolingbroke's double-dealing is implicit in the choice of words here. *Courtship* may be a serious attempt to gain affection, or mere bowing and scraping; *courtesy* can be an innate virtue, *la politesse du cœur*, or a formal curtsey ('Me rather had my hart might feele your loue, Then my vnpleased eie see your curtesie' Richard says to Bolingbroke at Flint Castle); *reverence* is likewise either the deepest regard or the outward sign of a respect which may or may not exist; and *craft* can be either the craftsman's admirable skill or a deplorable cunning. The last two lines can be interpreted in two ways. Either they mean 'making so light of his troubles that he seemed not to want people to worry about him'—the superficial appearance of Bolingbroke's behaviour—or they mean 'supporting great sorrow so bravely that he has taken their love into exile with him'—the actuality of the scene for both Bolingbroke and the populace. All the dangerous power of Bolingbroke's 'candied courtesy' is here made vivid in a few words.[1]

At Coventry, Gaunt protested that the king's words which should, in the nature of things, give life to their country, could deal only death; and at the beginning of Act II Gaunt himself dies, uttering with his last breath words which would be life to both king and kingdom if only Richard would heed them. We are made aware of the depth and weight of the language in this scene by the way Shakespeare has framed it between two pieces of dialogue in which words are identified with life: the opening quibbles on *breath* and *breathe*:

Gaunt. Wil the King come that I may *breathe* my last?
In holsome counsell to his vnstaied youth.
Yorke. Vex not your selfe, nor striue not with your *breath*,
For all in vaine comes counsell to his eare.

---

[1] If the lines are also taken to refer to Bolingbroke's conduct generally, and not only his leavetaking, 'underbearing of his fortune' can mean 'modest behaviour in spite of his high status'.

79

> *Gaunt.* Oh but they say, the tongues of dying men,
> Inforce attention like deepe harmony:
> Where words are scarce they are seldome spent in vaine,
> For they breathe truth that breathe their wordes in paine,
> (II.i.1-8)

and the announcement of Gaunt's death:

> *North.* My liege, old Gaunt commends him to your Maiestie.
> *King.* What saies he?
> *North.* Nay nothing, all is said:
> His tongue is now a stringlesse instrument,
> Words, life, and al, old Lancaster hath spent. (147-51)

The Sceptred Isle speech has a much richer meaning within this sharply-defined context than when it is extracted for a patriotic set piece, and it is worth seeing what are the elements that go to its composition. 'This earth of maiestie, this seate of Mars' fits in with the garden theme which is a *motif* of the play from its first hints in the opening scenes (Gaunt's pun about 'unstaied youth'—giddy, or unpropped—at the beginning of the present scene being one) to its full statement in Act III, scene iv. Here the garden is that of Eden[1] symbolic of security ('this fortresse built by Nature') and of fertility ('this happy breede . . . this teeming wombe of royall Kings'). But we do not expect to find Mars in Eden; and this same line—'This earth of maiestie, this seate of Mars' operates in another way by introducing a string of paradoxes and oxymora. *Earth* can be mere soil or the great globe itself,[2] *seat* is any stool till Mars makes it a throne, *stone* would be any pebble if the restrictive adjective did not make it a jewel. The effect is of something which might appear without value but is in fact of untold value, and 'this *dear dear* land' sharpens the paradox: what is dear in the sense that it is loved cannot be dear in the sense that it is priced for sale. By this time a third element has been introduced: England's rulers are

> Renowned for theyr deeds as far from home,
> For christian seruice, and true chiualry,
> As is the sepulchre in stubburne Iewry,
> Of the worlds ransome blessed Maries sonne. (53-6)

---

[1] Milton twice calls Paradise a happy seat.

[2] See a valuable article by Richard Altick: 'Symphonic Imagery in *Richard II*', *P.M.L.A.* LXII, pp. 339-65, which gives a full analysis of the play's images and shows how closely they are connected with its wordplay.

Gaunt may mean that some of England's kings have won fame fighting to regain Jerusalem, the kind of fame which his son will crave throughout his reign. But the grammatical ambiguity of the passage also yields the meaning that their virtues have made the English kings as famous as the sepulchre of Christ. Then, after the point at which most quotations end (short of a main verb), this King-Christ parallel, the garden-of-Paradise image and the paradoxes upon the theme of value are all brought together in a powerful climax:

> This land of such deare soules, this deere deere land,
> Deare for her reputation through the world,
> Is now leasde out; I dye pronouncing it,
> Like to a tenement or pelting Farme.　　　(57-60)

What is beyond all value has been valued and leased. The king, whose relation to his kingdom should be that of God to Paradise, who ought to 'regain the happy seat' has, instead of redeeming it (and here I suspect some Herbertish wordplay on the legal sense of *redemption*[1]), jeopardised its security and fertility by farming it out. The God-King analogy is a real one to Gaunt who has already been shown, in the second scene of the play, to have such belief in the divine right of kings that he 'may neuer lift An angry arme against his minister'. Yet he knows how little there is of the godlike in Richard's nature, and his bitter awareness of this gap between the ideal and the actual passes to the audience and later conditions our response to Richard's 'dear earth' speech over the land he has farmed out, or to his identification of himself with the betrayed and condemned Christ at a further stage of the drama.

From the profound wordplay of this speech to Gaunt's quibbles on his own name may seem a sharp descent; but the 'Gaunt as a grave' puns have a force which the king acknowledges when he asks 'Can sicke men play so *nicely* with their names?' *Nicely* means 'subtly' as well as 'trivially'. Gaunt's pun is not only true to the trivial preoccupations of the dying; it also reminds us of the play's dominant theme, the relationship between names and their bearers. Gaunt is saying in effect:

---

[1] It would be a concealed pun, but not the only one in the play. See J. Dover Wilson's note on V.i.13-15, and compare pp. 24-6 above.

'I am true to my name, Gaunt, but you are not true to the name you bear of King'. Besides this, *gaunt* in the sense of 'wasted' prepares us for his long speech of remonstrance, in which word-play underlines that relationship between the spiritual health of the king and the well-being of his kingdom which was a living concept for the Elizabethans, and which has been revived for us in the writings of modern anthropologists. Here the most telling puns are upon *possessed* and *verge*. If the king had attained self-government, were in possession of his kingdom of the mind, he would possess and not squander his wider inheritance; but the disorder of his mind within the verge (or rim) of his crown matches the external disorder that reigns through the *verge*—that part of the country, within a twelve-mile radius of the king himself, which fell immediately under the royal jurisdiction.

This by no means exhausts the puns with which Gaunt endeavours to pack the most meaning into the few words left for him to utter. But his efforts are in vain. Richard seizes Bolingbroke's estates and leaves for Ireland. Northumberland, Ross and Willoughby remain to sound each other's feelings from behind the cover of verbal ambiguities: 'My heart is *great* but it must *breake* with silence' says Ross, and the other lords take this in its oblique sense that his courage is high and he needs must speak his thoughts. Soon they are sure enough of each other to appreciate Northumberland's

> We see the wind sit sore vpon our sailes,
> And yet we *strike* not, but securely perish, (266-7)

and the scene ends with their resolve to

> Wipe off the dust that hides our Scepters *guilt*,
> And make high Maiestie looke like it selfe, (294-5)

which could be either a promise to reclaim Richard or a threat to overthrow him. It depends how we read *gilt*—and it is a pun which Shakespeare is seldom able to resist.

2

The scenes of Bolingbroke's progress through Gloucestershire and of Richard's landing in Wales balance each other in the play's symmetrical action. This is the point at which the

two buckets in a well pass each other. From Northumberland's
fulsome praise, we gather that Bolingbroke has beguiled the
tedium of their journey by the same charm of tongue that he
exercised upon the citizens at his departure. His reply to this
flattery is, however, short and meaningful: 'Of much lesse value
is my company, Then your good wordes.' Unlike Richard, who
believes in the extensional power of words and that the bearer
of them will really be paid on demand, Bolingbroke knows his
words of promise to his supporters to be pure speculation. There
is nothing in the bank, but if the speculation succeeds it will
bring him in a wealth of power and authority:

> all my treasury
> Is yet but vnfelt thanks, which more inricht,
> Shal be your loue and labours recompence.
> *Rosse.* Your presence[1] makes vs rich, most noble Lord.
> *Wil.* And far surmounts our labour to attaine it.
> *Bul.* Euermore thanke's the exchequer of the poore.
> Which till my infant fortune comes to yeares,
> Stands for my bounty.   (II.iii.60-7)

York's wordy rejection of his nephew's courtesies—

> grace me no grace, nor vnckle me no vnckle,
> I am no traitors Vnckle, and that word Grace
> In an vngratious mouth is but prophane   (87-9)

—implies what *Henry IV* confirms: that Bolingbroke's words
are in fact as blank as Richard's charters. Bolingbroke has,
however, enough military strength to carry York along with
him on the tide of rebellion; and by the time Bristol Castle is
taken, Bolingbroke's fair words have won him the power to
speak with regal authority in his sentence upon Bushy and
Green. His words, unlike those of Richard, are no sooner said
than done. The terse 'See them *dispatcht*' means 'Send them
away, see they are executed and hurry up about it'. Such is the
breath of kings—but such death-dealing is not the breath of
a true king; and the Pilate image with which Bolingbroke
washes his hands of the two minions' blood shifts our sympathy
towards Richard even while our admiration mounts for Bolingbroke.

[1] Ross plays insidiously on the commonplace and royal meanings of *presence.*

Meanwhile Richard has landed on the Welsh coast, unconscious of the fact that his glory is falling 'like a shooting star'
and confident in the belief that

> Not all the water in the rough rude sea,
> Can wash the balme off from an annointed King,
> The breath of *worldly* men cannot depose,
> The deputy elected by the Lord,
> For euery man that Bullingbrooke hath *prest*,
> To lifte shrewd steele against our golden *crowne*,
> God for his Ric: hath in heauenly pay,
> A glorious *Angell*; then if *Angels* fight
> Weake men must fall, for heauen still gardes the right.
>
> (III.ii.54-62)

The secondary meaning of *worldly*—'mercenary'—provokes a
shock of dissent with Richard's trust in his divine right. Worldly
men like Bolingbroke, who offer rewards, and worldly men like
Northumberland, who are hungry to be rewarded, can easily
depose the Lord's anointed. The monetary senses of *crown* and
angel, which are prompted by the sub-meaning of 'minted' for
pressed, sustain this threat that might, bought by the promise to
pay, is going to make short work of even divine right.

As the king's real power melts away in the disastrous news
brought by Salisbury and Scroop, he clings hard to the illusory
power of words: first to the power of his name:

> Is not the Kings name twenty thousand names?
> Arme arme, my name a puny subiect strikes,
> At thy great glorie;   (III.ii.85-7)

then to the worn consolations of philosophy, the trite 'sentences'
so fiercely rejected by Bolingbroke in his misfortunes:

> Say, is my kingdome lost? why twas my care,
> And what losse is it to be rid of care?   (95-6)

and then to the power of curses against those who have deserted
him:

> Would they make peace? terrible hel,
> Make war vpon their spotted soules for this.   (133-4)

Even these words are as futile as the Queen's vain curse upon
the gardener's plants, for Bushy and Green were not traitors.

Words cannot blow out facts, and finally, in a great speech, Richard acknowledges this. When he sits to tell sad stories of the deaths of kings he is no longer camouflaging hard truths with verbal fictions. He is admitting the discovery that the word and its referent are two things, the self-discovery that he is not all he has been called; although like the self-discovery of most of Shakespeare's tragic heroes this comes too late for disaster to be averted. This is Richard's real abdication. It is also in a sense his coronation, for he is made a king of griefs by a vision of human insignificance which carries him far beyond the discovery that the king is a man as other men are. Like Peer Gynt unpeeling the onion, Richard goes further than the man beneath the crown, to find the skull beneath the skin:

> within the hollow *crowne*
> That roundes the *mortall temples* of a king,
> Keepes death his *court*, and there the *antique* sits,
> Scoffing his state and grinning at his pompe,
> Allowing him a *breath*, a litle sceane,
> To monarchise be feard, and kil with lookes,
> Infusing him with selfe and vaine conceit,
> As if this flesh which wals about our life,
> Were brasse impregnable: and humord thus,
> Comes at the last, and with a little pin
> Boares thorough his Castle wall, and farewell King.
>
> (160-70)

Crown is both coronet and head, *temples* suggests the king's person (as in 'the Lord's anointed temple') as well as forehead; death is present not only as an external threat of disaster but as the inner inevitability. A further meaning of *temple* introduces the image of death presiding over a *court* of law as well as a royal court. There is an echo here of the verge image in Gaunt's reproaches to the king in Act II, and perhaps also a further echo of Marlowe's 'Death Keeping his circuit' in *Tamburlaine*, for Marlowe's metaphors are fresh in Shakespeare's memory when he is writing *Richard II*. The double meaning of *antic*, a clown as well as a gargoyle or death's head, leads to a further metaphor; the showman Richard finds life reduced to play-acting, a little scene, and that he too is a shadow in this kind. Death appears, as in the morality plays, with mops and mows

85

that parody the king's *mortal* authority. *Mortal* means 'subject to death' as well as 'deadly', and at the last the king's power is shown to be itself a parody and his life a mere breathing-space in the dance of death. The final image takes us back to the Sceptred Isle speech. England, bound in with the triumphant sea, is not impregnable against traitors; no divinity can hedge a king's person from the commonest enemy.

Wordplay and imagery here combine to give a poetic depth, rivalled only by the verse of *Macbeth*, to Richard's discovery that life has lost its meaning. The cliché implies, if we pause to ask what meaning here means, a philosophical experience of the first importance. Richard has discovered that words express only desires and not facts, that to call a man friend does not ensure the reality of friendship, that the name King, despite the sacramental nature of a coronation, does not imbue a man with kingly authority. If Richard were of the stature of Hamlet or Lear this tragic insight would remain clear even at the expense of his sanity, but his temperament cannot bear the sight of such bleak reality for long. He soon begins to draw round it the rags and shreds of appearance, to act the regal role once more—with this difference, that now he knows himself to be acting and that his words carry no effective weight. York's lines, spoken as Richard appears on the battlements of Flint Castle, help to emphasise this element of play-acting in the king's bearing:

> Yet lookes he like a King, beholde his eye,
> As bright as is the Eagles, lightens forth
> Controlling maiestie; alack alacke for woe,
> That any harme should staine so faire a *shew*.
>
> (III.iii.68-71)

The king is playing a part throughout the scene at Flint Castle, whether the role is that of offended majesty calling down vengeance upon those who dare to question his sovereignty or the role of a man disillusioned with pomp and power, willing to be buried in the king's highway. The elaborate verbal fancies—'I talke but idlely, and you laugh at me'—reveal that these speeches are not the real humility of Lear. They represent rather Richard's efforts to conceal his revelation from himself as well as others. His true feelings are exposed only for an instant in his cry to Aumerle:

> Oh that I were as *great*
> As is my griefe, or lesser than my name!   (136-7)

A greater character could bear the reality he has glimpsed and now tries to obscure with words; a character less great in the material sense, in authority and reputation, would never have suffered from the illusion that Richard has lost.

The deposition scene, for all its brilliance, adds very little to the total effect of the play. If *Richard II* was ever acted in the mutilated text represented by the first and second Quartos— and the long and rather irrelevant 'gage' scene which precedes the deposition reads like the padding to an abbreviated text— the loss, though serious, cannot have been structural, for the deposition only repeats the contrast, made in the scene at Flint Castle, between the reality of Richard's inward grief and its sham appearance in a profusion of words. From Richard's speech on entry—'Yet I well remember The *fauors* of these men' all the wordplay in the scene serves to intensify the theme of appearance and reality. 'Are you contented to resigne the Crowne?' Bolingbroke asks. Richard's reply:

> *I, no*; *no, I*: for *I* must nothing bee:
> Therefore *no, no*, for *I* resigne to thee,
>
>   (IV.i.201-2)

besides suggesting in one meaning (Aye, no; no, aye) his tormenting indecision, and in another (Aye—no; no I) the overwrought mind that finds an outlet in punning, also represents in the meaning 'I know no I' Richard's pathetic play-acting, his attempt to conjure with a magic he no longer believes. Can he exist if he no longer bears his right name of King? The mirror shows him the question is rhetorical but he dashes it to the ground, only to have Bolingbroke expose the self-deception of this histrionic gesture:

> The shadow of your Sorrow hath destroy'd
> The shadow of your Face.   (292-3)

It is true that the ritual of abdication invented by Richard, his rhetorical outbursts to Northumberland, the pantomime of the mirror, are all the shadows of his sorrow. In these speeches, Richard behaves as if words had value and effective meaning; whereas the substance of his sorrow is the unseen grief—unseen because undemonstrable—that no meaning is left in words. Bolingbroke has acted upon this knowledge ever since his banishment; and Richard's quibbles before the mirror weigh his own disastrous self-deception against Bolingbroke's politic deception of others:

> Is this the Face, which *fac'd* so many follyes,
> That was at last *out-fac'd* by Bullingbrooke?
>
> (285-6)

The long duel ends here in a curious sort of truce; both king and usurper now know there is no way of crossing the gulf between the world of words and the world of things. The knowledge has won the throne for Bolingbroke. It has also gained for Richard a kingly dignity he did not possess as king:

> You may my Glories and my State depose,
> But not my Griefes; still am I King of those. (192-3)

Richard retains this crown till the end of the play. The Elizabethan belief in the sanctity of kingship is not the only reason why the callow and capricious figure of the first acts is shown to die with the dignity of a martyr. Disaster has held up a mirror to Richard and in it he has glimpsed 'the truth of what we are'. He himself goes on playing with words, even alone at Pomfret; but at the motionless centre of this coloured wheel of language is the still and inescapable knowledge that it is all a play:

> Thus play I in one person many people,
> And none contented; sometimes am I King,
> Then treasons make me wish my selfe a beggar,
> And so I am: then crushing penurie
> Perswades me I was better when a king,
> Then am I kingd againe, and by and by,
> Thinke that I am vnkingd by Bullingbrooke,
> And strait am nothing. But what ere I be,
> Nor I, nor any man, that but man is,
> With nothing shall be pleasde, till he be easde,
> With being nothing. (V.v.31-41)

IV

THE SONNETS

The title of 'Shakespeare's Sonnets' must, in the year 1609, have met with a rather languid response. Here, ten years after the fashion had begun to fade, were somebody else's Sonnets; once again someone's heart and eye were at a mortal war, someone else's love was not so fair as fickle. One group of critics, with Sir Sidney Lee as its doyen, has revived this way of reading the Sonnets as exercises of wit rather than the overflow of powerful feelings. But for another, much larger number of readers the Sonnets are, as Gildon entitled them, 'Poems on Several Occasions'; not the flowers of rhetoric but the fruits of experience. Their interest is primarily biographical or even, since the Youth addressed in many of them was perhaps a public figure, historical.

Since the Sonnets are a very mixed lot, they include poems which lend support to either view of their composition. Some are so carefully ingenious that they suggest Shakespeare often sat down 'to write a sonnet' as resolutely as Tennyson did before breakfast. But their tortuous artifice makes them poor poems and goes a long way to justify the publisher who returned the series to Christopher Morley as not up to the literary standards of the house. Others appear to cry with the true voice of feeling. Although these are, to the biographer, by far the most interesting in the collection, they in their turn are seldom successful as poetry for the reason that Shakespeare, in writing them, was not sufficiently detached from the experience that gave rise to them to be able to watch all the forces of his mind at play. Yeats said that we make poetry of the quarrel with ourselves; but either the difference needs to be made up before we write the poem or, *qua* poet, we must referee the contest instead of fighting in it. The greatest Sonnets,

those which are neither wholly conventional nor wholly auto-
biographical, preserve this balance between embroilment and
detachment in a way which is truly dramatic. A personal
experience may underlie each, but it is experience transmuted,
as in the plays, into the correlative form of characters in action.
To some degree these characters are the dramatic counterparts
of actual people—the youth, the dark woman—though they
are not the people themselves. Others belong, as personages,
only to the microcosm of poetry: Time, for example, one of the
most powerful villains among Shakespeare's *dramatis personae*;
and above all, Shakespeare's own diverse masks and moods,
fully realised and understood:

> Where Sorrow is herself, forgetting all
> The gaucheness of her adolescent state.

If the best of the Sonnets thus stand in the same relationship
to Shakespeare's experience as do the plays, we can, without
drawing biographical inferences from the plays, make use of
them in our reading of the Sonnets. Thus one of the 'triangle'
sonnets, the forty-second, has its analogies in Shakespeare's
dramatic writing:

> Louing offendors thus I will *excuse* yee,
> Thou doost loue her, because thou knowst I loue her,
> And for my sake euen so doth she abuse me,
> Suffring my friend for my sake to *approue* her.

This has been variously interpreted as hard fact and pure
fancy. Although even Lee had to admit that it was not a
conventional theme for a sonnet, one anonymous nineteenth-
century critic found these sentiments so pusillanimous that
'this sonnet must be accepted as the expression of a friendship
existing in the imagination alone'. On the other hand, a more
recent critic psycho-analyses the lines to discover 'a fantastic
elaboration of what is known nowadays as the mechanism of
escape'.[1] The tone of the lines suggests, however, that Shakespeare here handles his own experience with exactly that blend
of implication and detachment that, as a dramatist, he communi-

[1] H. McC. Young, *The Sonnets of Shakespeare*: *A Psycho-Sexual Analysis*,
Columbia, Missouri (1937), p. 19. I have not been able to see the original and
quote from Hyder Rollins' *Variorum* edition.

cates to his audience, making us, in the plays, both share and survey a character's use of this 'mechanism of escape'. The situation arises when Lear seeks excuses for the failure of Regan and Cornwall to come and greet him, and when Desdemona, with even greater pathos, struggles to explain away Othello's first outburst of fury. The dramatic irony of the plays, where the audience knows the character to be wide of the mark, is matched in the sonnet by the irony with which Shakespeare contemplates himself excusing the inexcusable, and which is conveyed by the wordplay upon *excuse* and *approve*. *Excuse*, besides meaning 'make excuses, even where there is no justification for them' has the ironically impossible meaning of 'exculpate'; while if the youth *approves* the woman in the sexual sense, he can scarcely approve of her in the moral one. The incompatibility of these two sets of meanings explains as well as conveys Shakespeare's serene and witty detachment from the whole affair. The play on *excuse* shows that the youth's rivalry with Shakespeare's mistress troubles the poet far less than the sins of the spirit which he reproaches in more troubled sonnets, and the *approve* pun reflects Shakespeare's relief, after some anxiety, that the youth's behaviour is mere wild-oat experimentation and that he is not wasting high feeling on a woman whom the poet knows by experience to be little worth it. Shakespeare has understood the situation well enough to show his own role in it as a serio-comic one. No one could believe such fantastic rationalisations as are constructed here; Shakespeare himself mocks them, although he knows the unhappiness that constructs them.

The nature of the wordplay in the Sonnets varies according to whether Shakespeare is too remote or too near the experience behind the poem or whether he is at a satisfying dramatic distance from it. When he is detached, the wordplay is a consciously used, hard-worked rhetorical device. When his complexity of feeling upon the occasion of a sonnet is not fully realised by him, the wordplay often reveals an emotional undercurrent which was perhaps hidden from the poet himself. But in the best sonnets the wordplay is neither involuntary nor wilful; it is a skilfully handled means whereby Shakespeare makes explicit both his conflict of feelings and his resolution of the conflict.

1

Since the publication of *Astrophel and Stella*, readers had expected a fair measure of deliberately witty puns in a sonnet sequence, and many of Shakespeare's are this kind of embellishment. The first quatrain of the first Sonnet ends with a pretty paronomasia:

> From fairest creatures we desire increase,
> That thereby beauties Rose might neuer die,
> But as the riper should by time decease,
> His *tender heire* might *beare* his memory,

where the learned might spot a concealed Latin pun in *tender heir*; it was a bad one, but could be found in Holinshed, and Shakespeare was to use it later himself in *Cymbeline*:

> The peece of tender Ayre, thy vertuous Daughter
> Which we call Mollis Aer, and Mollis Aer
> We terme it Mulier: which Mulier I diuine
> Is this most constant Wife.   (V.v.447-50)

A similar pun on *husbandry* helps Shakespeare to ring rhetorical changes in the first seventeen sonnets on his advice to the young man to marry and have children. In many of these, Shakespeare's feelings are to some degree engaged, and the wordplay is structural and effective. But in less happy 'conceited' sonnets, the puns propel the thought instead of expressing it;

> Mine eye hath play'd the painter and hath steeld
> Thy beauties forme in *table* of my heart,
> My body is the *frame* wherein ti's held,
> And *perspectiue* it is best Painters art.   (24)

Shakespeare is here using knotty ambiguities to tie together odds and ends of conceits from other people's verse. The double senses of *table* ('writing tablet' and 'picture panel') and *frame* (bodily or picture frame), together with the various possible meanings of *perspective*, such as 'a picture frame', 'a framed lens through which to view objects', and 'the art of suggesting a third dimension on a two-dimensional surface', all serve to yoke by violence together such images as that of Ronsard:

> Il ne fallait, Maîtresse, autres tablettes
> Pour vous gravir que celles de mon cœur,

with Constable's:

> mine eye the window through the which thine eye
> may see my hart, and there thy selfe espy
> in bloody cullours how thou painted art,

and with Watson's:

> My Mistres seeing her faire counterfet,
> So sweetelie framed in my bleeding brest . . .

After such an ill-knit beginning it is not surprising that the poet gets into a hopeless tangle in the second quatrain:

> For through the Painter must you see his skill,
> To finde where your true Image pictur'd lies,
> Which in my bosomes shop is hanging stil,
> That hath his windowes glazed with thine eyes.

Are the windows of this last line the poet's eyes through which the friend looks into his heart? If so, they cannot also belong to the Painter busy inside the shop. But if they are the eyes of the image which the poet carries in his heart, the friend must be looking into his own inside. Whatever sense we try to make of the passage, the resultant image is pure Bosch, an anatomical horror; and while it must be allowed that the best images are often the least picturable, it is difficult not to visualise an image taken from the visual arts. In other unsuccessful sonnets, Shakespeare's habit of hoisting himself up by a word's double meaning when his poetic élan fails him results, not in confusion as here, but in a mechanical consistency. Sonnet 46 begins with the most conventional of poetic themes:

> Mine eye and heart are at a mortall warre,
> How to deuide the *conquest* of thy sight.

In a dogged attempt to give novelty to the theme, Shakespeare seizes upon the legal meaning of *conquest*—'the personal acquisition of real property otherwise than by inheritance', and turns the poem into an elaborate forensic allegory with the help of further puns on *side*, meaning 'to decide' and also 'to assign to one of two sides or parties', and on *quest* in its chivalric meaning of adventurous search and its legal sense of 'inquiry upon the oaths of an empanelled jury'. Love as a lawsuit can never have had, even for the litigious Elizabethans, any of the poetic force of love conceived as war, and this conceit upon a conceit palls long before we have reached the end of the sonnet.

In the first of these examples the image was enforcedly pictorial, and in the second it was elaborately consistent. But Shakespeare's most telling imagery is scarcely ever visual; and it is nearly always made complex by such a fusion of ideas as occurs in Lady Macbeth's 'Was the hope drunke Wherein you drest your selfe?' Such imagery as this abounds in the finest of the sonnets, where the wordplay, instead of serving to multiply unrealised images, gives verbal cohesion to images which are already fused in the heat of Shakespeare's imagination. The opening of Sonnet 2 is an illustration:

> When fortie Winters shall beseige thy brow,
> And digge deep trenches in thy beauties *field*,
> Thy youthes proud liuery so gaz'd on now,
> Wil be a totter'd *weed* of smal worth held.

Three senses of *field*, a battlefield, an agricultural field, and the surface of a shield, together with *weed* as both tare and dress, serve to bring the figure of Time the Warrior into association with the more powerful and traditional personification of Time the Reaper, and so prepare us for the sestet of the sonnet. Time reaps, but he also sows; by begetting children the youth can be new made when he is old. The same figure of the Reaper enters Sonnet 116, and here the function of the second, inadmissible meaning of *compass* together with the wordplay of *bear out* (which might mean 'steer a course') is to keep before us in the sestet the octave's powerful navigation image, which might otherwise be effaced by the double personification of Love and Time:

> Let me not to the marriage of true mindes
> Admit impediments, loue is not loue
> Which alters when it alteration findes,
> Or bends with the remouer to remoue.
> O no, it is an euer fixed marke
> That lookes on tempests and is neuer shaken;
> It is the star to euery wandring barke,

Whose worths vnknowne, although his higth be taken.
Lou's not Times foole, though rosie lips and cheeks
Within his bending sickles *compasse* come,
Loue alters not with his breefe houres and weekes,
But *beares it out* euen to the edge of doome:
    If this be error and vpon me proued,
    I neuer writ, nor no man euer loued.

The same cluster of images recurs in Sonnet 60, and here again
the wordplay helps to fuse the metaphors into an imaginative
whole:

Like as the waues make towards the pibled shore,
So do our minuites hasten to their end,
Each changing place with that which goes before,
In sequent toile all forwards do contend.
Natiuity once in the *maine* of light,
Crawles to maturity, wherewith being *crown'd*,
Crooked eclipses gainst his *glory* fight,
And time that gaue, doth now his gift confound.
Time doth transfixe the *florish* set on youth,
And delues the *paralels* in beauties brow,
Feedes on the rarities of natures truth,
And nothing stands but for his sieth to mow.
    And yet to times in hope, my verse shall *stand*
    Praising thy worth, dispight his cruell *hand*.

By contrast with the awkward huddle of images at the beginning
of Sonnet 24, the start of this is controlled and steady; the first
image of minutes as waves is displayed slowly, as if to reassure
the reader and win his co-operation for the complex movements
of thought which follow in the second and third quatrains. In
the fifth line, the word *main* connects the opening image of the
sea with the shining sphere of light into which a planet is
launched at its ascendant, while *crawls* reflects back on nativity
a second meaning of 'child'. In the double image of the infant
on the floor and the sun mounting the heavens there is just that
blend of the mundane and the cosmic which constitutes the
feliciter audax of Shakespeare's mature style—we meet it
everywhere in *Antony and Cleopatra*—and the unity of the
images is kept by the double meaning of *glory* which is both an
aureole and the pride of manhood. *Crooked*, in its figurative
sense of 'malignant' belongs to the astrological figure, while its

literal sense evokes the pictorial image of the sliver of an eclipsed sun, curved like a scythe, and so leads us inevitably to the figure of Time the Reaper in the third quatrain. Conversely, *parallels* (in line 10), by recalling the lines of latitude on a celestial globe, harks back to the astrological image. *Flourish* may retain its original meaning of the blossom on a fruit tree, which would give a subsidiary sense to *crown'd* (the crown is the leafy part of a tree); the dominant meaning of *flourish* is probably the figurative one of vigour, prime, perfection, but the calligraphic sense—'a decoration or ornament achieved with a sweep of the pen'—prepares us for the poet's defiance of Time's *hand* in the last couplet; and here the dead metaphor in *stand* is resuscitated to suggest that Shakespeare's praise of his friend is one thing too tough for Time's scythe.

2

Sonnet 49 will furnish a vivid example of wordplay which reveals an unresolved and painful tension in Shakespeare's feelings for his friend:

> Against that time (if euer that time come)
> When I shall see thee frowne on my defects,
> When as thy loue hath *cast* his vtmost *summe*,
> Cauld to that audite by *aduis'd respects*,
> Against that time when thou shalt *strangely* passe,
> And scarcely greete me with that sunne thine eye,
> When loue conuerted from the thing it was
> Shall reasons finde of setled grauitie.
> Against that time do I insconce me here
> Within the knowledge of mine owne *desart*,
> And this my *hand*, against my selfe vpreare,
> To guard the lawfull reasons on thy part,
>> To leaue *poore* me, thou hast the strength of lawes,
>> Since why to loue, I can alledge no cause.

The second quatrain of this is the rejection of Falstaff in little. The parallel is strengthened by the sun image (as in Hal's 'Yet heerein will I imitate the Sunne') and by the way *gravity* calls to mind the Lord Chief Justice's reproach to Falstaff: 'There is not a white haire on your face, but shold haue his effect of grauity.' And our divided feelings towards Hal in his premeditated rejection of his old companion are exactly matched by the divided feelings revealed in the wordplay of this sonnet. What distresses the poet about his friend and what distresses us about Hal is not the inevitable gesture of repudiation, but the cold deliberation with which it is prepared. The image of the third line is one of calculation, if we take the words to mean: 'reckoned up your expenditure of affection'. But there's beggary in the love that can be uttered; and the phrase *cast his utmost sum* can also suggest a love that is poured out without counting upon any return, a love such as the poet has lavished on the youth. *Advised respects* in the next line is glossed by Palgrave 'considerations formed by reflection', and, taken in this sense, the words imply a kind of rueful admiration; but they can also mean 'a prompted, or suggested, consideration of our respective social positions', which would be something far less admirable although, in the late sixteenth century, not easy to evade. While the unemotive meaning of *strangely*—'as a stranger'— represents Shakespeare's effort to understand and justify his friend's coldness, the emotive meaning of the word voices his hurt bewilderment. At the same time, the ambiguity of *deserts* (compare 'As to behold desert a begger borne', in Sonnet 66, with Hamlet's 'Vse euerie man after his desart, and who should scape whipping?') shows that the poet's self-abasement has its reservations. In the penultimate line some critical bitterness blends with the abject tone if we read *poor* as cause rather than effect of the writer being abandoned. Finally, the grammatical uncertainty of the last line, taken together with the various meanings of *cause*, sums up all Shakespeare's turmoil of feelings towards his friend. 'I cannot produce any assertible claim for your love. But my love for you is generous, uncalculating, unrestrained, for who can give a lover any law? And if I do not meet with an equally strong love in you, if you are as cold and calculating as I sometimes fear, my love will be without justification.'

This fear that his friend is not worth all the affection that he has spent upon him finds an outlet in unconscious puns in other sonnets: in, for example, the phrase: 'Thou best of *deerest*, and mine onely *care*' in Sonnet 48, or in the opening of Sonnet 67: 'Ah wherefore with infection should he liue', where the implication that the friend is indeed a lily that has festered is not quite effaced by the next line: 'And with his presence grace impietie?' 'Th' expence of Spirit in a waste of shame' is to Shakespeare a less painful, because a more clearly understood, experience than this expenditure of love upon someone whom we, with him, suspect to be a brilliant, prudent, calculating egotist. In the plays some of the anguish of this situation is reflected in Antonio's devotion to Bassanio in *The Merchant of Venice* or that of another Antonio (the identity of names is telling) for Sebastian in *Twelfth Night*. The bitterness which underlies the submerged wordplay of many sonnets invades and nearly shatters the comic mood of *Twelfth Night* when Antonio, mistaking Viola for Sebastian, thinks he has been abandoned by his friend:

> Let me speake a little. This youth that you see heere,
> I snatch'd one halfe out of the iawes of death,
> Releeued him with such sanctitie of loue;
> And to his image, which me thought did promise
> Most venerable worth, did I deuotion.
>
> .   .   .   .   .
>
> But oh, how vilde an idoll proues this God:
> Thou hast Sebastian done good feature, shame.
> In Nature, there's no blemish but the minde:
> None can be call'd deform'd, but the vnkinde.
> Vertue is beauty, but the beauteous euill
> Are empty trunkes, ore-flourish'd by the deuill.
>
> (III.iv.395-406)

A fear such as this, that the friend he has entertained for a Horatio because he seems not to be passion's slave, may in fact be an Angelo, makes Sonnet 94 one of the most involved and difficult in the sequence:

> They that haue powre to hurt, and will doe none,
> That doe not do the thing, they most do showe,
> Who mouing others, are themselues as stone,
> Unmooued, could[1], and to temptation slow:
> They rightly do inherrit heauens graces,
> And husband natures ritches from expence,
> They are the Lords and owners of their faces,
> Others, but stewards of their excellence:

[1] i.e. *cold*. There is a very full discussion of this Sonnet in W. Empson's *Some Versions of Pastoral* (1935), pp. 89-115.

The sommers flowre is to the sommer sweet,
Though to it selfe, it onely liue and die,
But if that flowre with base infection meete,
The basest weed out-braues his dignity:
   For sweetest things turne sowrest by their deedes,
   Lillies that fester, smell far worse then weeds.

If this is praise, it is the most back-handed of compliments, for
there is doubtful merit in being cold like a stone and in the
narcissic self-enjoyment of living and dying to oneself. The
antithesis of lord and steward is another teasing image, for it
suggests that the paragon who is the object of all this praise has
appropriated talents which are lent and not given. There is here
an undercurrent of warning: such a warning as the Duke speaks
to Angelo at the beginning of *Measure for Measure*:

            Thy selfe, and thy belongings,
Are not thine own so proper, as to waste
Thy selfe vpon thy vertues; they on thee
Heauen doth with vs, as we, with Torches doe,
Not light them for themselues: For if our vertues
Did not goe forth of vs, 'twere all alike
As if we had them not: Spirits are not finely touch'd,
But to fine issues: nor nature neuer lends
The smallest scruple of her excellence,
But like a thrifty goddesse, she determines
Her selfe the glory of a creditour,
Both thanks, and vse.

                    (I.i.29-40)

Measure for Measure seems to me a great but unsatisfactory play
for the same reason that Sonnet 94 is, on its own scale, a great
but unsatisfactory poem: in each case Shakespeare is emotionally
too involved in the situation to achieve a dramatic clarification
of its issues. He was perhaps drawn to the existing versions of
the *Measure for Measure* story by the dramatic potentialities in
the character he calls Angelo: the self-centred, self-sufficient
man who makes a tragic discovery of his own weakness. The
story, however, compelled Shakespeare to make the centre of
interest the clash between Angelo's hypocrisy and Isabella's
integrity whereas the play's fundamental conflict is less a
moral than a psychic one, and is summed up in the confrontation
of the Duke's Innocent-the-Third asceticism in the 'Be absolute

for death' speech with the affirmation of life in Claudio's outcry: 'I, but to die, and go we know not where!' A play can quite well embody a psychic alongside a moral conflict, but here the two issues do not correspond. Shakespeare is on Isabella's side in the moral conflict, since he and his audience believe the soul matters more than the body; but he cannot side with her in the psychic conflict because virginity could never seem to him the positive good it appeared to Spenser and Milton. For Shakespeare there could be no doubt that it was better to live and give life than to die, or to live in a way that amounted to a refusal of life. Right at the end of the play, Shakespeare manages to identify Isabella with the affirmative principle by having her ask pardon and life for Angelo. But until then, that principle has to make itself felt in other ways; in, for instance, the nearly silent figure of Juliet serenely carrying Claudio's child, or in the tolerant treatment of Pompey—'a poore fellow that would liue'.

Sonnet 94, like several others in the series, originates from a similar confusion of feelings. Shakespeare, who has himself been a motley to the view, is torn between admiration for those who are able to keep themselves detached and seemingly unspotted from the world, and the misgiving that such people may be incapable of the good passions as well as the bad. The equipoise of admiration and distrust is especially delicate in the first seventeen sonnets, written, if we can trust the chronology of the sequence, while the youth's self-sufficiency still appeared wholly virtuous and the poet had not yet discovered that 'suns of the world may stain'. There is repeated play in these first sonnets upon the word *use*, because its three main senses— 'employment', 'wear and tear' and 'usury'—suggest a contemporary moral dilemma which acts as a vivid metaphor of Shakespeare's divided feelings towards his friend. It had long been forbidden by the Church, on the authority of Scripture, to make money breed by taking interest for it; but changing economic conditions were driving the Elizabethans to find scriptural warrant for the practice in such passages as the Parable of the Talents. That story, echoed in the speech already quoted from *Measure for Measure*, and in Sonnet 94, is also recalled in Sonnet 11:

> Looke whom she [that is, nature] best indow'd,
>   she gaue the more;
> Which bountious guift thou shouldst in bounty cherrish.

Repeatedly, through these first seventeen sonnets, Shakespeare thus makes use of the contemporary bewilderment over the ethics of usury to define his own torn emotions about his friend. Fear of the other's inherent selfish coldness makes him urge the youth to put his gifts to use by marrying and begetting children:

> Profitles *vserer* why doost thou *vse*
> So great a summe of summes yet can'st not liue?   (4)

> That *vse* is not forbidden vsery,
> Which happies those that pay the willing lone.   (6)

> Looke what a vnthrift in the world doth spend
> Shifts but his place, for still the world inioyes it
> But beauties waste hath in the world an end,
> And kept *vnvsde* the *vser* so destroyes it.   (9)

Another powerful pun through which Shakespeare conveys, on the one hand, his grudging admiration for his friend's self-sufficiency and, on the other, his longing that he may show some readiness to give himself, is that on *husband* and *husbandry*. In what sense was it meritorious to 'husband natures riches from expence'? *Husbandry* can mean saving, economy, as in Banquo's 'There's Husbandry in Heauen, Their Candles are all out', or it can mean the outlay of cost and labour that brings forth the fruits of the earth. An association through metaphor of this last meaning with the theme of marriage—as in Enobarbus's 'He plough'd her and she cropp'd'—strengthens the association of ideas through wordplay:

> Who lets so faire a house fall to decay
> Which *husbandry* in honour might vphold?   (13)

The paradox that only by spending can we save, which underlies Shakespeare's use of *husbandry* and *usury*, is expressed in yet another image in Sonnet 5:

> Then were not summers distillation left
> A liquid prisoner pent in walls of glasse,
> Beauties effect with beautie were bereft,
> Nor it nor noe remembrance what it was.
>   But flowers distil'd though they with winter meete,
>   Leese but their show, their substance still liues sweet.

The same metaphor is to be met with in *A Midsummer Night's Dream*, where Theseus warns Hermia that if she does not concur with her father's wishes she must live as a vestal virgin:

> Chanting faint hymnes to the cold fruitlesse Moone,
> Thrice blessed they that master so their blood,
> To vndergo such maiden pilgrimage,
> But earthlier happie is the Rose distil'd,
> Than that which withering on the virgin thorne,
> Growes, liues, and dies, in single blessednesse.
>
> (I.i.73-8)

The image here suggests the same conflict between traditional moral or religious ideas and strong personal feelings grounded on experience which is found in *Measure for Measure*. Traditionally, the rose plucked stood for present pleasure, and we should expect the rose distilled to stand (as in Herbert's *The Nose-gay*) for the treasure laid up in heaven. The vital opposition for Shakespeare, however, is not between earthly and heavenly, but between the selfish and the generous; and he identifies procreative love with the rose distilled. The meanings given to the word *virtue* in the Sonnets accord with the same distinction. Virtue is not the cold disinclination to passion such as is seen in those who are lords and owners of their faces; it is an active principle, like the *virtue* or healing property of plants and precious stones. The final couplet of Sonnet 93, immediately preceding 'They that have power', makes full play with these meanings:

> How like Eaues apple doth thy beauty grow
> If thy sweet *vertue* answere not thy show.

At the worst, as Shakespeare here implies, the youth's cool self-possession masks a corrupt heart. And at the best it makes him no better than the canker-roses of which he writes in Sonnet 54:

> But for their *virtue* only is their show,
> They liue vnwoo'd, and vnrespected fade,
> Die to themselues. Sweet Roses doe not so,
> Of their sweet deathes, are sweetest odors made.

Shakespeare's feelings about his friend are for the most part too confused to make a shapely sonnet. The interplay of mixed feelings in the sonnets on the woman, on time and poetry, and on the rival poet, are conflicts understood and expressed with a confident wit. But the complex relationship of the poet and the youth is further involved with other relationships: that of player to rich patron and, since the youth represents many things Shakespeare lacks and craves in his own personality, Shakespeare's quarrel with himself. When Shakespeare thus unlocks his heart, it is to reveal its stores in disarray. In only a few of the poems addressed to the youth are these stored experiences ordered into a work of art.

3

The difficulty confronting us at this point is that any separation of the successful from the unsuccessful sonnets is bound to seem, at worst, an arbitrary and very personal choice and, at the best, to be based on criteria which are not universally acceptable. Thus John Crow Ransom distinguishes as goats among the sonnets the 'associationist' ones which provide 'many charming resting-places for the feelings to agitate themselves', and, as sheep, the 'metaphysical' sonnets which go 'straight through to the completion of the cycle and extinction of the feelings'.[1] For Mr Ransome, wordplay belongs to the poetry of association, and so the punning sonnets are among the unsuccessful ones. This view is, of course, based on a strictly kathartic theory of poetry; but probably the poetic theory more generally acceptable today is nearer to that of the seventeenth-century Aristotelians: the belief that poetry should communicate feeling, but feeling purified by being fully and finally comprehended—in fact, all that is summed up in Herbert's definition of prayer as 'The land of spices; something understood'. If this is our criterion, we shall look first in a sonnet, not for the kind of logic which could be reduced to a prose syllogism, but for a satisfying organisation of sound and sense that conveys the ordered movement of thought into which the emotion has been shaped.

The Shakespearean sonnet is not an easy form to handle. In an Italian form of sonnet, even one which, like Milton's 'On his Blindness', does not keep strictly to the divisions of octave and

[1] 'Shakespeare at Sonnets' in *The World's Body* (N.Y. 1938), p. 291.

sestet, there is a marked ebb and flow of thought corresponding to two emotional impulses: in that case, despair and resignation. But the final couplet of the English sonnet is too brief to contain the entire counter-statement to the first three quatrains without giving the impression that the poet is trying to wrench the poem back on its course. If, however, the poet too anxiously anticipates the final turn of thought throughout the first twelve lines, the couplet loses its epigrammatic spring. A subdued sort of wordplay is a useful device to the poet in these circumstances. It allows him to introduce the counter-movement of thought before the reader is aware of its presence, so that the final couplet satisfies both by conscious surprise and by its fulfilment of a subconscious expectation. This is what happens in Sonnet 63:

> Against my loue shall be as I am now
> With times iniurious *hand* chrusht and ore-worne,
> When houres haue dreind his blood and fild his brow
> With *lines* and wrincles, when his youthfull morne
> Hath *trauaild* on to Ages steepie night,
> And all those beauties whereof now he's King
> Are vanishing, or vanisht out of sight,
> Stealing away the treasure of his Spring.
> For such a time do I now fortifie
> Against confounding Ages cruell knife,
> That he shall neuer *cut* from memory
> My sweet loues beauty, though my louers life.
> > His beautie shall in these blacke lines be seene,
> > And they shall liue, and he in them still greene.

The turn accomplished by the couplet from the theme of time destroying the youth's beauty to that of its preservation through poetry is skilfully prepared, throughout the preceding quatrains, by an oblique image of Time (or Time-Age, a composite figure) and the poet working in competition one with the other. Time defaces the young man's beauty by scribbling upon it or overscoring it, at the same time as the poet is making of it a speaking picture for posterity. This theme of writing or engraving is implicit in the subsidiary meanings of *hand* in line two, *lines* in line four, and *cut*, which can mean engrave ('This figure that thou here seest put, It was for gentle Shakespeare cut'). *Trauaild*, one of Shakespeare's favourite portmanteau words, packed with the two meanings 'travelled' and 'travailed', helps here by introducing the ideas of effort; the poet's toil undoes the result of life's weary journey through time.

In Sonnet 65, the couplet's counter-statement is again carefully prepared in the preceding lines:

> Since brasse, nor stone, nor earth, nor boundlesse sea,
> But sad mortallity ore-swaies their power,
> How with this rage shall beautie hold a plea,
> Whose *action* is no·stronger then a flower?
> O how shall summers hunny breath hold out,
> Against the wrackfull siedge of battring dayes,
> When rocks impregnable are not so stoute,
> Nor gates of steele so strong but time decayes?
> O fearefull meditation, where alack,
> Shall times best Iewell *from* times chest lie hid?
> Or what strong hand can hold his swift foot back,
> Or who his *spoile* of[1] beautie can forbid?
> > O none, vnlesse this miracle haue might,
> > That in black inck my loue may still shine bright.

The first four lines of this would be a strong rhetorical question, compelling our assent, were its compulsion not weakened by the double meaning of *action*; for while the action of beauty, taking the word in the sense of 'physical force', cannot compare with the resistance of brass and stone, the legal meaning of 'a process', induced by *plea* in the preceding line, hints that physical strength cannot deflect the course of justice and of the justicers above. There is a sense in which both flowers and summer are stronger than rocks, because they are endlessly renewed while rocks are continually eroded away; and with this in mind, we can read both lines three to four and lines five to eight as exclamations, rather than as rhetorical questions compelling a negative answer. The second quatrain can then be paraphrased: 'How successfully the renewing vitality of summer resists the assaults of time! Unassailable rocks and gates of steel are not as strong as it; on the contrary, time itself wears away.' And once our consent to these rhetorical questions has been weakened in this way, without our being aware of it, there may be some hesitation about our response to the next question:

[1] For 1609 *or*.

105

O fearefull meditation, where alack,
Shall times best Iewell *from* times chest lie hid?

The ambiguity of *from* imparts two meanings to this: either 'Where can the best jewel that Time has produced out of his casket be hidden?' or 'Where can Time's jewel be hidden away so that it may not be put back into Time's chest, the grave?' Put in this second form, the question produces the inevitable answer that the youth's soul and body will be preserved by their immortality from Time—'the womb of all things and perhaps their grave'. This undertone is sustained by the quasi-religious language of 'fearful meditation' and 'miracle', by the harrowing-of-hell notion in 'gates of steel' and by the opening lines' Apocalyptic imagery. Herbert would have developed this undertone into the poem's counter-statement, but Shakespeare is concerned with the immortality bestowed by art, and uses the religious theme only to make the reader receptive to his final claim. The ambiguity of *spoil* helps. It may mean 'spoiling', the ruination of time; but it suggests also precious plunder— gold and jewels—which is indestructible and in safe keeping. So the whole sonnet subtly prepares us for the claim made in the last couplet.

Another formally satisfying sonnet, the thirtieth, also uses an elaborate play of meaning to anticipate its confident end:

> When to the Sessions of sweet silent thought
> I sommon vp remembrance of things past,
> I sigh the lacke of many a thing I sought,
> And with old woes new waile my *deare* times waste:
> Then can I drowne an eye (vn-vs'd to flow)
> For *precious* friends hid in deaths dateles night,
> And weepe a fresh loues long since *canceld* woe,
> And mone th'*expence* of many a vannisht sight.
> Then can I greeue at greeuances *fore-gon*,
> And heauily from woe to woe *tell* ore
> The sad *account* of fore-bemoned mone,
> Which I new *pay* as if not *payd* before.
> > But if the while I thinke on thee (*deare* friend)
> > All losses are restord, and sorrowes end.

Sweet sets the tone of this in the first line. Shakespeare's melancholy is well-savoured. 'Summon' suggests that he is too

judiciously detached from his memories for them to be painful
to him, and this detachment is implicit in *dear*, *precious*, *cancelled*,
expense, *tell*, *account*, *pay*. Besides their strongly felt meanings,
these words all have neutral meanings which are as impersonal
as book-keeping entries; *expense*, for example, means primarily
'the price paid', whereas in 'Th'expence of spirit' this meaning
is subordinate to the emotive one. Even when an emotion is
stated, the tone of the verse dissipates the force of the statement.
'Then can I greeue at greeuances fore-gon' has the suggestion
of 'I could upset myself—if I tried'; the verbal jingle robs the
line of any solemnity, and grievances *forgone* are repudiated
and forgotten as well as simply past. This is not the anguish of a
Francesca over past happiness in days of misery, but the con-
templation of old misfortunes in a happy time. Shakespeare's
eye, in fact, is kept on the credit side of the ledger all through
the poem, and when the *dear* friend is produced at the last we
understand why this reverie over disaster has been far more
sweet than bitter.

The sonnets in which Shakespeare's conflict of feelings is
most clearly understood and so most poetically organised are
the ones about the rival poet and these addressed to the dark
woman. The poet is clearly an adversary whose skill Shakespeare
respects at the same time as he is convinced of the superior
strength and sincerity of his own verse, and these counterpoised
feelings dance an ironic set of changes in a sonnet such as the
eighty-fifth, which begins:

> My toung-tide Muse in manners holds her *still*,
> While comments of your praise richly compil'd
> Reserue their Character with goulden quill,
> And *precious* phrase by all the Muses fil'd.

According to the meanings we give *still* and *precious*, this says
either: 'My Muse keeps silent as becomes her when other poets
write so exquisitely well in your praise', or: 'My Muse, by
her reticence, remains well-mannered whatever excesses of
affectation other poets may commit in their praise of you.'
Irony is pushed a stage further in the sonnets to the woman.
Whereas the equivoques addressed to the youth are veiled by
tact and compassion, those to the mistress are brutally obvious.

She is 'rich in *Will*', 'the wide worlds *common* place', 'the *baye* where all men *ride*'. The only satisfying thing for Shakespeare about this infatuation with a light woman who has not even acknowledged beauty to commend her, is that each perfectly understands and accepts the other's deception and self-deception. The theme of Sonnet 138 might be summed up in the refrain of a recent poet as 'You know I know you know I know you know'.[1] Its insight not only makes it a more coherent poem than most of those addressed to the youth but also, if we allow love poetry more scope than the posy to a ring, one of the finest love poems:

> When my loue sweares that she is made of truth,
> I do beleeue her though I know she lyes,
> That she might think me some vntuterd youth
> Vnlearned in the worlds false subtilties.
> Thus *vainely* thinking that she thinkes me young,
> Although she knowes my dayes are past the best,
> *Simply* I credit her false speaking tongue,
> On both sides thus is *simple* truth supprest:
> But wherefore sayes she not she is vniust?
> And wherefore say not I that I am old?
> O loues best *habit* is in seeming trust,
> And age in loue, loues not t'haue yeares *told*.
> Therefore I *lye* with her, and she with me,
> And in our *faults* by *lyes* we flattered be.

Faults has a double meaning to enforce the wordplay on *lie*; it means both the lovers' adultery and their deception of each other. As Patrick Cruttwell says: 'Of this climactic poem the last couplet, with its pun on "lye" is the very apex; the pun forces together the physical union and its context, as it were, its whole surrounding universe, of moral defilement and falsehood.'[2] Yet the total impression of the sonnet is not one of bitterness, but of acceptance. The lovers need one another in their common weakness.

Only a few of the sonnets to the youth show an irony as fully realised and as moving as this. Sonnet 87, which concludes the Rival Poet sequence, allows a pensive understanding of the youth's calculating temper to show through its seeming self-abasement:

---

[1] Thom Gunn, 'Carnal Knowledge'.
[2] 'A Reading of the Sonnets', *Hudson Review V* (1952), pp. 563-4.

> Farewell thou art too *deare* for my possessing,
> And like enough thou knowst thy *estimate*,
> The Charter of thy *worth* giues thee releasing:
> My *bonds* in thee are all determinate.

Here the play of meaning between 'valuable' and 'beloved' for *dear*, 'your valuation of yourself' and 'the amount of my esteem' for *estimate*, 'value' and 'worthiness' for *worth*, and 'claim' and 'shackle' for *bond*, offers distinct and conflicting readings of the whole passage. Either Shakespeare is saying: 'You are so good and great that you may well end our friendship on the ground that there is no corresponding worth in me', or he means: 'Because of your social advantage over me, you exact too high a price for our friendship, so I have decided to break free.' In addition, there is a strong hint of the meaning: 'I have lavished affection on a creature who is just not worth it.' Shakespeare is in fact recording the terrible moment of apprehension when he means all these at once. A tone of guarded compliment masks his feelings in the following lines of the sonnet, but this profound disillusionment breaks through in the final couplet:

> Thus haue I had thee as a dreame doth flatter,
> In sleepe a King, but waking no such matter.

The irony here is grave and steady; in Sonnet 58, where a compliment is likewise framed in two ironic statements, the tone is one of exasperation: 'That God forbid, that made me first your slaue' evokes the natural protest that the speaker was not created any man's slave, and this sting remains even when we have grasped the fact that this god is Cupid. Its smart is still felt in the final couplet, which may be the voice of a man prostrate with adoration or of one querulous with impatience—'You think this is what I am made for, do you?'

> I am to waite though waiting so be hell,
> Not blame your pleasure be it ill or well.

The hectic tone of this suggests a strong tension of feelings. There is more calmness and deliberation in the preceding sonnet, the fifty-seventh, which will serve as a final example of Shakespeare's verbal precision in defining the interplay of mixed feelings:

Being your slaue what should I doe but tend,
Vpon the *houres*, and times of your desire?
I haue no precious time at al to *spend*;
Nor *seruices* to doe til you require.
Nor dare I chide the world without end houre,
Whilst I (my soueraine) watch the clock for you,
Nor thinke the bitternesse of absence sowre,
When you have bid your seruant once adieue.
Nor dare I question with my iealious thought,
Where you may be, or you affaires suppose,
But like a sad slaue stay and thinke of nought
Saue where you are, how happy you make those.
 So *true* a foole is loue, that in your *Will*
 (Though you doe any thing) he thinkes no ill.

Lines three and four are a little obscure. We might paraphrase: 'I have no strong claims on my time and attention except yours'. But *spend* can have a more forceful meaning of 'expend' or even 'waste' and this insinuates an unexpected note of protest: 'Time is too valuable for me to waste it in this fashion'. The ecclesiastical senses of *hours* and *services* and the echo of the doxology in 'world without end' serve to buttress the counterstress set up by this protest; Shakespeare resents the time he has squandered upon a false devotion. And once this note of resentment has been struck, its reverberations are heard in the over-strong protestations of 'Nor dare I chide . . .' and 'Nor dare I question'. The extent to which Shakespeare does chide and question is shown in the last two lines of the sonnet which appear to say: 'Love is so foolishly faithful in your Will Shakespeare that he cannot think ill of you, whatever you do'; but which also say: 'Love is so utterly foolish that, however wilful and perverse you are, it cannot see the wrongness of your behaviour.' In depicting this blend of adulation and contempt, and in all those sonnets where verbal ambiguity is thus used as a deliberate dramatic device, Shakespeare shows that superb insight into states of strangely mixed feelings which enabled him to bring to life a Coriolanus or an Enobarbus. Like Freud, he found the causes of quibbling by studying his own quibbles; and the detachment which such an analysis implies imparts to the best of the Sonnets that objectivity we look for in the finest dramatic poetry.

V

HAMLET

One evening's total loss of memory, in which he might enjoy *Hamlet* as a new play, would perhaps be the greatest boon that could be granted to a reader of Shakespeare. Many wise and illuminating things have been said about the play; but there are times when one would relinquish every line of *Hamlet* criticism in order to sweat with the expectation of the Ghost's arrival on the battlements or to gasp at the unexpectedness of his appearance in Gertrude's closet, to share Hamlet's feverish hope that Claudius may walk into the Mousetrap, or to grow tense at the thought that Hamlet might do it pat now that the king is at his prayers. A good performance can still give us some taste of these thrills and apprehensions, but through long familiarity the drama has lost for us the excitement of a real mystery play.

To the Elizabethan audience, it must have been primarily a mystery drama in the cinema-poster sense of the word. It is a detective story: almost everyone in it is involved in some form of detection. Horatio, Marcellus and Bernardo seek to discover the cause of the Ghost's hauntings, Polonius has no difficulty in getting from Ophelia the key of her memory and sets spies on his son Laertes, Old Norway discovers the real reason for Fortinbras's levy of forces, Rosencrantz and Guildenstern probe Hamlet's melancholy and Ophelia is used as a decoy to bring its causes to light, Hamlet tricks the King into self-exposure by having the players re-enact his crime before him, Polonius eavesdrops with fatal results, Hamlet at sea finds out the plot against his life, Laertes returns secretly to Denmark and lurks about the court to discover who is guilty of his father's death. The task laid upon Hamlet by the Ghost belongs to this level of the play's action. A crime has been committed. It is for

111

the victim's son to detect the murderer and bring him to the wild justice of revenge.

Hamlet is also a mystery play of a deeper kind. It is a mystery play in the medieval sense and its background of a Catholic eschatology keeps us constantly in mind of something after death. Murder and incest are unnatural acts; but behind and beyond the discovered crimes lies an evil which is supernatural —'there is somthing in this more then naturall, if Philosophie could find it out'. Philosophy however (as Hamlet tells Horatio) does not comprehend mysteries of this order. Hamlet's own insight into such mysteries sets him apart from friends and enemies alike. Everyone else is concerned in the unmasking of legal crimes. Hamlet alone, surrounded by the politic ferrets of a Machiavellian court, knows that the action in which he is involved is

> not a story of detection,
> Of crime and its punishment, but of sin and expiation.

The wrong suffered by Hamlet is not a mere tarnish that may be wiped from his scutcheon. It is something he feels as an ineradicable corruption in the nature of life itself. Before the Ghost reveals to Hamlet a crime which cries out for retribution, Hamlet has himself discovered through his mother's conduct a guilt which makes retribution impossible because irrelevant. Nothing can be done, and Hamlet does nothing.

There can be nothing novel in this statement of what appears to me to be the dominant theme of *Hamlet*, since there cannot be, on the waveband of speculation, room for any new theory of Hamlet's inability to act. I can only defend this interpretation as one which emerges from the study of the play's language: from its imagery and particularly from its dominant images as they have been studied by Wolfgang Clemen[1] and from its wordplay as it has been brought into its right prominence by J. Dover Wilson in his edition of the play. A lot could be said about the puns and ambiguities of *Hamlet*, which has more quibbles than any other of Shakespeare's tragedies. Here however I am ignoring many aspects of the wordplay in order to

---

[1] *The Development of Shakespeare's Imagery* (1951), pp. 106-18.

show how it contributes to the dramatic realisation of a psychological conflict: the conflict between the demands of an accepted ethical code and Hamlet's particular vision of evil.

1

Francisco's few words before he leaves the platform help a good deal to build up the first scene's atmosphere of tense disquiet. His 'You come most *carefully* vpon your houre' implies Bernardo's anxiety as well as his own pleasure in being relieved of his watch. 'Sick at hart' also can be made to suggest something more than nausea from the biting cold. Like all good mystery writers, Shakespeare trails some red herrings at the beginning of his work: the watchers on the platform are convinced that the Ghost has come to forewarn Denmark of some great military disaster. But like all good mystery writers Shakespeare also drops us a fine and subtle clue which will thicken as the play proceeds. Horatio fears that the apparition 'bodes some strange *eruption* to our *state*'. Ostensibly this means an outbreak of violence in the life of the country, but the pathological sense of *eruption* ('tetter') and the possibility of *state* referring to the individual's state of health as well as to the body politic prepare us for the disease imagery of later parts of the play; and in this conjunction of the two meanings, the public and the particular, we have a first faint sounding of the play's major theme.

This first elusive statement is picked up by another instrument in Claudius's speech at the beginning of the Court scene which follows. Thinking his '*state* to be disioynt, and out of frame', Claudius has taken his brother's widow to be 'Th'imperiall ioyntresse to this warlike *state*'. The meaning 'condition of an individual' is present, in that Claudius's spiritual state is most certainly out of frame, but it is not consciously with us if we are hearing the words for the first time. For this is a State occasion in the national sense of the word; everyone is wearing his public face and observing court etiquette. After so much ceremonious speech-making, Hamlet's first words have outrageous force, for he begins as he is to continue, a man talking to himself.

The first encounter of Hamlet and Claudius in this scene is a verbal duel equal in skill and excitement to the fencing match of the last act. Each character puns in such a way as to make his meaning clear to his opponent and yet beyond the bystanders' comprehension. It soon becomes clear that each has different grounds for his hostility. Claudius directs his insinuations against Hamlet's supposed resentment at being ousted from the direct succession; Hamlet's attack is levelled at Claudius's marriage to Gertrude within the prohibited degrees. Thus Claudius's first words: 'But now my Cosin Hamlet, and my sonne' are meant to be conciliatory, since 'son' implies 'heir', but Hamlet's muttered rejoinder: 'A little more then kin, and lesse then *kind*', in which *kind* means 'in the family', 'according to natural law' and 'affectionate', defines his bitterness at his mother's match. When Hamlet replies to the King's: 'How is it that the clowdes still hang on you?' with: 'Not so my Lord, I am too much in the *sonne*',[1] he wraps inside a compliment about the King's favour the statement that he is insulted to be called Claudius's son; whereas Claudius takes the reply to mean that Hamlet considers himself dispossessed, out of house and home. The Queen senses the hostility in this first passage of arms, as can be seen in her appeal to Hamlet:

> Doe not for euer with thy *vailed* lids
> Seeke for thy noble Father in the dust,

where *vailed* means not only 'lowered' (as a flag is vailed), but also *avaled*, having the beaver down ready for combat. His reply takes up the meaning of *veiled* as 'disguised' and hints that his grief is not simulated, although hers may well be:

> Tis not alone my incky *cloake* good[2] mother
> Nor customary *suites* of solembe blacke
> Nor windie suspiration of *forst* breath
> No, nor the fruitfull riuer in the eye,
> Nor the deiected hauior of the visage

---

[1] All quotations from the play are from the second Quarto (facsimile of the Huntington Library copy, 1938) except when, as here, there is good reason for preferring the Folio reading. In this case the Quarto printer anticipated 'much' and produced 'Not so much my Lord . . .'

[2] From the Folio. The Second Quarto has *coold*.

Together with all *formes, moodes, shapes*[1] of griefe
That can denote me truely.   (I.ii.77-83)

Each word italicised here is ambiguous and can suggest an
assumed disguise as well as the outer manifestation of genuine
qualities. The sincerity is Hamlet's, the pretence Gertrude's.
Claudius meanwhile has had time to ponder Hamlet's *in the
sonne*, and in consequence his own trite attempt to cheer
Hamlet up ends with words of menacing equivocation:

> for your intent
> In going back to schoole in Wittenberg,
> It is most *retrogard* to our desire,
> And we beseech you *bend* you to remaine
> Heere in the cheare and comfort of our eye,
> Our chiefest courtier, cosin, and our *sonne*.   (112-7)

The phrase 'we beseech you bend you to remain' can mean
either 'we beg you to be so inclined as to stay' or 'we beg you,
nay, we *compel* you to stay'. *Retrogard*, or *retrograde*, is an
astrological term meaning 'contrary to the usual motion of the
planets' and *bend* can also have an astrological sense as in
Milton's 'Bending one way their precious influence'. These
terms of astrology, taken with Hamlet's previous quibble,
bring *sun* simultaneously to mind with *son*. When we recall
how instinctively the Elizabethan mind associated the king and
the sun (as in *Henry IV*), we find that Claudius is saying in
effect: 'You may think that because you are the rightful heir
you can travel about acting the Pretender; but it is I, the actual
ruler, who have freedom of action and control all by my
influence, and I am determined to keep you stationary—like
the earth.'

In this way Claudius reveals to us his fears of Hamlet's public
grievance that he has been thrust out of the direct line of succession. But once the King and his courtiers have left the stage,
the real cause of Hamlet's grief erupts in the cry: 'O that this
too too sallied[2] flesh would melt!' 'That within which passes
shewe' is not his sorrow for his father, which can be outwardly

---

[1] Fourth Quarto's correction of the second Quarto's *chapes*. The Folio has
shewes.   [2] i.e. sullied. See above, pp.15-16

expressed, but a violent realisation of evil, born of his mother's conduct in forgetting Hyperion for a satyr. Her action is Eve's first sin; it has left Hamlet feeling deeply tainted in his own nature in that he is the son of woman.

Horatio's report of the Ghost breaks into this black despair, and Hamlet arranges to join the watchers on the platform. The reflections he there makes, before the Ghost appears, on the drunkenness of the Danes, add nothing to the action and, to judge by the Folio, they were cut out in the acting. But in its play of meanings the speech is vital to our understanding of Hamlet's dilemma:

> This heauy headed reueale east and west
> Makes vs tradust, and taxed of other nations,
> They clip vs drunkards, and with Swinish phrase
> Soyle our *addition*, and indeede it takes
> From our atchieuements, though perform'd at height
> The pith and marrow of our *attribute*,
> So oft it chaunces in particuler men,
> That for some vicious *mole* of nature in them
> As in their birth wherein they are not guilty,
> (Since nature cannot choose his origin)
> By their *ore-growth* of some *complextion*
> Oft breaking downe the pales and forts of reason,
> Or by some *habit*, that too much ore-leauens
> The forme of plausiue manners, that these men
> Carrying I say the stamp of one defect
> Being Natures *liuery*, or Fortunes *starre*,
> His vertues els be they as pure as grace,
> As infinite as man may vndergoe,
> Shall in the generall censure take corruption
> From that particuler fault: the dram of eale
> Doth all the noble substance of a doubt
> To his owne scandle.   (I.iv.17-38)

The direct, surface meaning of this speech contrasts oddly with the soliloquy of the second scene. Hamlet, who has let us see his own vision of an ineradicable evil now laments the fact that men who are 'as pure as grace' are counted ill-doers because of some superficial blemish in their characters. But underlying meanings in Hamlet's words unify the two speeches. *Addition*, besides being our applied title, is the sum total of our natures,

116

what we add up to in ourselves. *Attribute*, according to the *N.E.D.*, can mean not only a quality ascribed or assigned but an inherent or characteristic quality. Since the *mole* as a burrowing animal is in Shakespeare's mind before this episode of the play ends ('Well sayd olde Mole'), it is not perhaps too far-fetched to indicate, in the word's use here, a nuance of 'something that undermines from within' as well as the obvious meaning of a surface blemish. According to whether we take *complexion* to mean the colouring of the skin or an inherent disposition of mind, *o'er-growth* means either 'a spreading over the surface' or 'excessive enlargement'. Fortune's *star* may be a skin-deep characteristic, like the blaze or star in a horse's forehead, and this meaning is possibly induced by *livery*, which can be 'provender' as well as 'official dress'—the kind that hides our true appearance; but its more obvious meaning is the disposition with which, thanks to our stars, we are born. Together, all these conflicting senses of Hamlet's words voice the fundamental question of the play and the problem that confronts Hamlet himself: is evil superficial, a mere deflection of humanity from its position as 'the beautie of the world; the paragon of Animales' or is it the very condition of our birth? And because 'You can't turn bread to dough again', the image implicit in *o'er-leavens* points to its being ineradicable.

These shadow meanings make the lines a structural unit in the play rather than a rhetorical set speech, and they are dramatically placed. As soon as Hamlet has let us see, through these manifold ambiguities, his recognition of a wrong that cannot be righted, the Ghost appears and commands him to right a wrong. The duty imposed upon Hamlet is the public one of exposing and revenging the crimes of regicide and adultery that stain the Danish royal house:

> Let not the royall bed of Denmarke be
> A couch for luxury and damned incest.   (I.v.82-3)

But in the moment that he demands vengeance from his son, the Elder Hamlet renders action impossible for him by deepening his sense of an evil that no human intention can purify; first in the tale of his own purgatorial sufferings and secondly in the revelation that Gertrude's adultery took place during her first husband's lifetime. Hamlet's dilemma is symbolised in the Ghost's description of his murder; he feels not only the surface disfigurement to his family honour—the 'most instant tetter'—but knows his strength to be vitiated by an inner poison which

> doth posset
> And curde like eager droppings into milke
> The thin and wholsome blood.[1]   (I.v.68-70)

How is he to rid the state of Denmark of an usurping murderer when the state of all humanity is so deeply polluted, when, in Lear's phrase, 'None does offend' because existence itself is the prime offence? It is useless for the Ghost to say:

> Tain't not thy minde, nor let thy soule contriue
> Against thy mother ought, leaue her to heauen,
>   (I.v.85-6)

since Hamlet's mind is already tainted as his flesh is sullied, and his soliloquy which follows the Ghost's departure shows that he is as much obsessed with his mother's guilt as with his uncle's crime: 'O most pernicious woman'. The 'trivial fond records' that he wipes from his tables are exactly those ethical commonplaces he now needs if he is to carry out the Ghost's commands. He knows that the law of nature and of nations would justify his killing Claudius. He knows also that evil is not so easily rooted out of society; the unweeded garden has run to seed and no amount of weeding can prevent the growth of what has already seeded. No action that Hamlet can take will restore his mother's innocence.

2

There is no one to share Hamlet's burden. Although we gather that he tells Horatio of the Ghost's revelation, the man who is not passion's slave is not one who can understand Hamlet's deepest disquiet, and his one attempt to express his feelings to Rosencrantz and Guildenstern is met by knowing smiles. Hamlet must keep silent; silent about his profoundest

---

[1] *Posset* is the Folio's correction of the second Quarto's *possesse*. Professor Clemen was the first to show the full significance of the image.

griefs because they are incomprehensible to others, silent about
his knowledge of the murder lest the King forestall his revenge.
The first act stresses this need for silence: 'Breake my hart,
for I must hold my tongue'; 'Giue it an vnderstanding but no
tongue'; and the act ends with Hamlet swearing his friends to
secrecy about the Ghost. But unless his heart is to break, his
feelings must find some outlet; and from the beginning of the
second act they seek one in the fantastic wordplay of his antic
disposition.

Other characters pun besides Hamlet. Polonius is quibbling
the first time we find him playing the fool in his own house:

> thinke your selfe a babie
> That you haue tane these *tenders* for true pay
> Which are not sterling, *tender* your selfe more dearely
> Or (not to crack the winde of the poore phrase
> Running[1] it thus) you'l *tender* me a foole.
>
> (I.iii.105-9)

But these foolish figures are introduced chiefly for their dramatic
contrast to Hamlet's puns. Whereas Hamlet's wordplay releases
his deepest feelings, Polonius's is largely a rhetorical affectation of the court. Only occasionally do his less deliberate quibbles reveal something of the man's nature, as when he says to
Ophelia:

> Doe not belieue his vowes, for they are *brokers*
> Not of that *die* which their *inuestments* showe
> But meere implorators of vnholy *suites*
> Breathing like sanctified and pious *bonds*
> The better to beguile.   (I.iii.127-31)

A *broker*, besides being a go-between, could be a second-hand-
clothes dealer, and Polonius's delight in disguise and mystifi-
cation makes him develop this second meaning in the lines which
follow: *dye* is 'colour of cloth' as well as 'appearance', *invest-
ments* are garments and also 'sieges', the *suits* are both sets of
clothing and causes or requests, and there may even be a
suggestion of 'a clergyman's bands' (*band* and *bond* being

[1] Collier's emendation. The Quartos have *Wrong* and the Folios *Roaming*.

alternative spelling[1]) for the pious *bonds* which are ostensibly the written undertakings of a lover's vows. All Polonius's love of sleuthing on the trail of policy is implied by the wordplay of such a passage. With his erudition about the classical drama and his experience of acting a Brute part in the university, Polonius embodies the social code of the older type of revenge play from which *Hamlet* has developed—and diverged; a social code that has grown meaningless to Prince Hamlet, although he struggles to act on its dictates. The contrast of these two outlooks is suggested at the beginning of the second act when Polonius, whose business in life is to play the 'politician', tries to discover the misdeeds of Laertes by having Reynaldo lay slight sullies on his son. A sully is a mere surface tarnish to Polonius; but Hamlet, who has discovered misdeed in plenty in his own family, feels himself to be polluted by his discoveries. One result of this is that his antic wordplay arises more often from his quarrel with himself than from his quarrel with the King.

The verbal fencing of Claudius's first encounter with Hamlet continues, however, through the middle acts of the play. It suits Hamlet to menace the King with his supposed ambition for the throne up to the time that the play-scene reveals his knowledge of the murder. So the King's conciliatory: 'How *fares* our cosin Hamlet?' is met by

> Excellent yfaith,
> Of the Camelions dish, I eate the *ayre*,
> Promis cram'd, you cannot feede Capons so.
> (III.ii.97-100)

Rosencrantz and Guildenstern are rebuffed with a similar insulting wordplay. They are Hamlet's *dear* friends, because he knows they have been offered expensive bribes to watch him, and he takes perversely their 'Wee'l wait vpon you'[2] to mean 'We'll be your servants.' But he will not sort them with the rest of his servants because he is most *dreadfully attended*; words which not only imply that he is spied upon from all sides, or that he is not over-pleased by *their* presence (meanings which

---

[1] *N.E.D.*, however, gives no instance earlier than the end of the seventeenth century. [2] From the Folio. The passage is not in the Second Quarto.

relieve his feelings), but that he has not the attendants that, as rightful King, he should have—a meaning he intends them to report to Claudius. The phrase also takes us back to the deeper level of Hamlet's experience by bringing to mind the Ghost. These defensive-aggressive quibbles show that Hamlet knows a hawk from a handsaw. On the surface, this is simply: 'I am no fool, I know chalk from cheese.' It also means, since a *hawk* is some kind of tool and *handsaw* a quibble on *heronshaw*, that Hamlet recognises his school-fellows as the King's tools, sent after him as birds of prey are loosed in the royal sport of falconry.[1]

Besides these deliberate and provocative puns that indicate Hamlet's concern with his social duty of revenge, there are others, more numerous and spontaneous, which express the inner desperation that keeps him from that revenge for so long. The unhappy nonsense verse of so unhappy a poet as A. E. Housman shows how attempted nonsense can give the rein to our profoundest anxieties; and when Hamlet cries: 'I could accuse mee of such things, that it were better my Mother had not borne mee . . . what should such fellowes as I do crauling betweene earth and heauen?' he voices a real and not an assumed revulsion against human nature. In the play scene, when Hamlet is consciously preoccupied by his external duty of watching the King's every word and gesture, the same revulsion finds a spontaneous outlet in his bitter innuendoes towards Ophelia and, through her, towards the Queen; innuendoes which, like Hamlet's use of *nunnery* in an earlier scene, become the more outrageous when we discover how much of Hamlet's language here consists of *double-entendre* which the Elizabethan audience would have recognised for what it is, although the modern actor skates nimbly over it.[2] At times Hamlet's word-play does double duty by both masking his hostility towards Claudius and affording him a safety-valve for his bitterness at his mother's guilt. The words, 'Conception is a blessing, But as your daughter may *conceaue*, friend looke to't', are meant to

---

[1] This intricate pun is elucidated by J. Dover Wilson in his edition, pp. 179-80.
[2] Alec Guinness's 1951 Old Vic Hamlet was an exception, but the critics did not like it.

throw Polonius on to the wrong scent and so safeguard Hamlet against the King's suspicions. They also spring from the mood in which he curses the hour wherein he was born.

Such wordplay offers Hamlet only a temporary relief from an intolerable position, from the snakehold of that mortal *coil* which is an isolated pun illuminating the whole play. Behind the word's superficial, contextual meaning of 'commotion, turmoil' lies, in the idea of a coil of rope, an image of convolution as powerful as Blake's Mundane Shell. It suggests the labyrinthine ingenuity with which Claudius and Polonius go about and about to pluck out the heart of Hamlet's mystery; the maze of his own mind; the temporal-spatial restrictions of mortal life, seen by the Elizabethans as the concentric spheres of the physical world; above all, the corruption of mortal flesh which Hamlet longs to slough off as a snake its skin. One obvious way out of this tragic impasse is in his mind from his first appearance in the second act when he parries Polonius's 'Will you walke out of the ayre my Lord?' with the quibbling 'Into my graue'. There may be aggressive quibbling on both sides here. Polonius might be saying (though it is rather too subtle for him): 'Won't you stop being "too much in the sun"?' And Hamlet may be quibbling on *heir-air* to imply: 'I shall, as heir, not cease to be a menace to the King until I am dead.' The chief effect of Hamlet's pun is, however, to give vent to his own world-weariness. But, in his reflections upon suicide, death presents itself as a consummation *devoutly* to be wished; and the word serves to conjure up the whole afterlife conceived by the devout. The evil that Hamlet perceives does not stop with death, and since the Everlasting has 'fixt His cannon gainst self slaughter' suicide would only perpetuate, by unpardonable sin, the corruption that he feels in his own nature.

One other way of escape suggests itself to Hamlet and is implicit in the same soliloquy. The dead travel to an *undiscovered* country; undiscovered not only in being unrevealed, undisclosed to the living, but also in the sense that we have no proof that those who began the journey ever reached their goal. It is not that Hamlet has forgotten the Ghost, but that he does not want to believe in him. The safest refuge from the kind of moral

shock Hamlet has sustained is a sweeping scepticism. Evil can
be averted by denying it objective existence: 'for there is nothing either good or bad, but thinking makes it so'. Hamlet doubts
the Ghost, not because he shirks the action the Ghost demands
of him—he does not hesitate to kill Polonius when he mistakes
him behind the arras for the King—but because the Ghost's
sufferings and knowledge of Gertrude's lightness have confirmed that sense of nature's depravity from which he longs to
be freed. Even at the moment of the meeting on the ramparts,
Hamlet wants to doubt the Ghost whose revelation he fears
with all his prophetic soul:

> Thou com'st in such a *questionable shape*
> That I will speake to thee.   (I.iv.43-4)

Questionable means not only 'that I may question' but also
'doubtful, uncertain', and *shape*, besides being the essential
form of something, has more commonly in Shakespeare the
meaning of a theatrical costume or disguise.[1] The whole
passage from which the words are taken is deeply expressive of
Hamlet's uncertainty about the Ghost's real nature—is it a
spirit of health or a goblin damned?—which Dr Wilson believes
to be the real cause for his delaying his revenge until the Ghost's
honesty has been put to the test by the play-scene. But for this
to be so, the audience would have to share Hamlet's doubts
whether the Ghost is devil or spirit; and even a modern audience
with little or no serious belief in either devils or spirits believes
every word the Ghost says. So, while the Ghost is actually
speaking, does Hamlet. And in subsequent scenes it is not his
doubts about the Ghost which give rise to his inability to act,
but his inability to act which gives rise to his scepticism about
the Ghost. *The Murder of Gonzago* is staged to catch Hamlet's
own conscience as well as the King's. By a vivid portrayal before
his own eyes of the circumstances in which his father died,
Hamlet seeks to recapture the resolution with which he at first
met the Ghost's command. Yet in this re-enactment, as in the
soliloquy which conceives it, there is a good deal of neurotic
self-torment. Hamlet's state of mind is very like that of Troilus

[1] See above, pp. 54-5

at the sight of Cressida's infidelity; he cannot take his eyes from a sight so appalling, yet he cannot believe his own eyes:

> Let it not be beleeu'd for womanhood:
> Thinke we had mothers.

After the play-scene, our interest shifts for a time to the King and Gertrude. There has been some exaggerated white-washing of Claudius in recent discussion of the play. We can be sure that to the Elizabethans he was a villain, and a nasty villain at that. But one of the play's most interesting features is the curious parallel between the experiences of Hamlet and those of his uncle up to their almost simultaneous deaths. Like Hamlet, Claudius suffers from a divided mind. He too has a social role to fill, and performs it well from his first admirable conduct of the kingdom's affairs in the opening act. He handles the Fortinbras episode firmly, and shows real courage when Laertes bursts into the palace with a rabble at his heels. But beneath this assurance lies a particular guilt as corrosive as Hamlet's generalised experience of human corruption:

> The harlots cheeke beautied with plastring art,
> Is not more ougly to the thing that helps it,
> Then is my deede to my most painted word:
> O heauy burthen. (III.i.51-4)

Like Hamlet, the King can take no action that will free him. Hamlet's despair at the mortal coil is matched by Claudius's cry: 'O limed soule, that struggling to be free, Art more ingaged'. The prayer-scene completes this ironic identification of the mighty opposites. Hamlet could kill Claudius now and the eye-for-an-eye code of honour would be satisfied. Laertes would cut *his* enemy's throat in the church, although to do so would presumably jeopardise his own soul and might dispatch his victim's in a state of grace to heaven. But the Ghost's revelations of the afterlife have made Hamlet aware of the inadequacy of such a revenge. He does not know that Claudius's prayers are also inadequate, 'words without thoughts'; so that at this encounter hero and villain are one in their despair at the incompatibility between a real evil and the token action which pretends to remedy that evil. The same ironic identification of

the antagonists is made when Claudius, in yet another image of
disease, speaks of Hamlet as an infection in the body politic:

> We would not vnderstand what was most fit,
> But like the owner of a foule disease
> To keepe it from divulging, let it feede
> Euen on the pith of life.   (IV.i.20-3)

The words reflect back on the bloat King; he is the rottenness
in the state of Denmark. But they have also some real relevance
to Hamlet, since he has let his vision of evil feed on the pith of
life, until it has become impossible for him to eradicate the
particular evil of Claudius enjoying his father's crown and his
father's wife.

Claudius has a conscience, and in that he is a worthy antag-
onist for Hamlet. Gertrude, on the other hand, seems, like
Augusta Leigh, to have 'suffered from a sort of moral idiocy
since birth'. Hamlet is attempting the impossible when, in the
closet-scene, he tries to make Gertrude see the enormity of her
behaviour. The shock of Polonius's death has done something
to break down Gertrude's defences, and for a moment Hamlet
succeeds in compelling her to share his own valuation of her
actions:

> O Hamlet speake no more,
> Thou turnst my very eyes into my soule,
> And there I see such blacke and greined[1] spots
> As will leaue there their tin'ct.   (III.iv.88-91)

Gertrude's nature is too weak, however, to sustain the full
force of Hamlet's revelation. The Ghost on his appearance not
only protects her from Hamlet's eloquence with the reminder
that 'Conceit in weakest bodies strongest workes'; he also
gives scope for the conceit, much stronger than remorse, that
Hamlet, talking to vacant air, is so indubitably mad that his
reproaches can safely be ignored and forgotten. Her utter incapacity to share Hamlet's vision is summed up in her words:
'All that there is I see.' And after the Ghost has vanished,
Hamlet accepts this incapacity in words which record the
beginning of that wisdom which comes to nearly every one of

[1] Folio reading. The second Quarto has *greeued*.

Shakespeare's tragic heroes. Hamlet is not Shakespeare's weakest hero but his strongest, and never stronger than when he here discovers that average humanity can never share his vision of a naked evil, but needs the shelter of those pretences which have become so transparent to his own way of seeing. So he bids Gertrude: 'Assume a vertue if you haue it not'—

> And when you are desirous to be *blest*,
> Ile blessing beg of you.   (171-2)

Experience has shown Hamlet that there is often a vast difference between *blessed* in the sense of 'having received a benediction' and meaning 'in a state of salvation'. The second does not necessarily or generally follow upon the first. But now, with a new humility, he conforms with the appearance of things, and after all his mockery of accepted relationships—'We shall obey, were she ten times our mother'—comes to accept a parental blessing from an unblest parent. Although the speech marks the beginning of Hamlet's recovery from his despair, its sudden clarity and charity are quickly clouded over by either a revulsion of feeling or fear lest Gertrude reveal his sanity to the King; and the scene closes with Hamlet reassuming his antic disposition in the last of his quibbles at Polonius's expense: 'Come sir, to *draw toward an end* with you.'

3

Shakespearean criticism is at present wary of an over-romanticised, world-weary Hamlet, the anachronistic victim of our modern *Angst*. But while it is true that Hamlet's mind is furnished with many concepts that belong only to the sixteenth century, the language of the play reveals, in imagery and wordplay, an emotional experience which cannot alter as long as the basic relationships of mother, father and son persist. I have here taken Hamlet's word for it that he does procrastinate in his revenge; and I have taken what appear to me to be Shakespeare's words for it that he is impeded by the sense of an ineradicable wrong, by the corruption in existence itself. If Hamlet remained in this despondency, the play would be a pathological study and not a tragedy. To remain fixed in the Hamlet experience would be to become incurably insane. The dramatic interest of Hamlet lies less in the fidelity with which Shakespeare has recorded his melancholy than in the way Hamlet himself transcends this melancholy in the play's last act. At the end of the play the division in Hamlet's mind, between his social obligation to avenge a crime and his discovery of 'an instant eternity of evil and wrong',[1] is healed, and he is able to act, although not before the King has taken decisive and fatal action against him. One movement towards such a recovery is made in the closet scene. Another had begun even earlier, with the arrival of the players and Hamlet's reflections upon the Player's Hecuba speech.

During the greater part of the play, action is impossible for Hamlet because it seems to him that to kill the King would be a mere histrionic gesture without any real effect upon the course of nature. Yet circumstances force Hamlet, who can see through all the pretences of social codes and conventions, to dissimulate as much as anyone in the play, first by acting the role of madman and then by making use of the players to prepare his trap for the King. There may be a good deal of personal feeling embedded in this paradox. If the discovery of a bad reality under a good appearance was a vivid experience to Shakespeare about this time (and plays like *Troilus and Cressida* and *Measure for Measure* suggest that this was the case), his own career as an actor must have seemed deception itself. Yet as a playwright, Shakespeare knew that in an Aristotelian sense the drama could be more 'real' than the flux of life which it imitated. So Hamlet finds that the fact that all the world's a stage does not free anyone from the obligation to play his destined part. When the part is played out and Hamlet addresses those

> that looke pale, and tremble at this chance,
> That are but mutes, or audience to this *act*,
>
> (V.ii.348-9)

there is more to the image than that artistic bravura with which Shakespeare dares make the Egyptian queen fear some squeak-

---

[1] *Murder in the Cathedral*, p. 77. All T. S. Eliot's first three plays deal with the Hamlet experience, but their solutions of it are less dramatically satisfying than *Hamlet* itself.

ing Cleopatra shall boy her greatness. Hamlet's play upon *act* show that in performing his part of the avenger he has at last closed the intolerable gulf between appearance and reality; and the image itself symbolises this by breaking the illusion of the audience just at the kathartic moment when the action it has witnessed is known to be more real than the events of yesterday and tomorrow.

From the time Hamlet begins his journey to England, all occasions spur him to action. First there is the example of Fortinbras. Then, once at sea, Hamlet has to move quickly to evade the plot laid against him:

> Or[1] I could make a prologue to my braines
> They had begun the play.   (V.ii.30-1)

The action he takes exactly parallels that of Fortinbras; he assumes, without a moment's misgiving, the authority of his dead father. In the play's sequence of scenes, we learn of this activity only after the scene in the graveyard, and that episode, at the beginning of Act V, is vital in effecting Hamlet's recovery of the power to act. His quibbles over the bones are his last and most embittered statement of the discrepancy between appearance and reality which has kept him inactive for so long:

> This fellow might be in's time a great buyer of Land, with his Statutes, his Recognizances, his Fines, his double Vouchers, his Recoueries: Is this the *fine* of his *Fines*, and the *recouery* of his *Recoueries*, to haue his *fine* Pate full of *fine* Dirt? will his Vouchers *vouch* him no more of his Purchases, and double ones too, then the length and breadth of a paire of *Indentures*?[2]

The particular and the individual, profession and rank, are all confounded in the dust that stops a beer barrel, and the common fate makes vanity vain: 'Now get you to my Ladies table, and tell her, let her paint an inch thicke, to this fauour she must come.' And then, to end this mood for good and all, Ophelia's funeral procession comes into sight. Ophelia does not in her lifetime play a very important part in Hamlet's story, but the

---

[1] i.e. *ere.*

[2] From the Folio, which restores the passage between the two 'Recoveries' jumped by the Quarto's printer.

dead Ophelia is able to transform Hamlet from the figure of human consciousness pondering the vanity of human wishes to an individual affirming his particular role in time and circumstances;

> this is I
> Hamlet the Dane.   (V.i.279-80)

Ophelia, now he has lost her, is no longer Woman to be derided as the original source of corruption, but the unique object of unique feelings:

> I loued Ophelia, forty thousand brothers
> Could not with all theyr quantitie of loue
> Make vp my summe.   (V.i.291-2)

This acceptance of circumstances and of a role, however meaningless it may seem, that he is called to play in them, is completed when Hamlet tells Horatio that the readiness is all. Hamlet's fate cried out to him at his first encounter with the Ghost, but until this conversation with Horatio before the fencing match he is unable to answer that cry. And when he is at last ready, his enemies too are ready, Laertes with his venomed foil, Claudius with his union pearl full of poison. Only when his own minutes are numbered is Hamlet able to leave all his other problems to Providence and, accepting the intolerable fact of his mother's union with Claudius, to assume his destined part of the avenger; and this consent to his destiny is sealed with one of Shakespeare's most meaningful puns:

> Heere thou incestuous, murderous, damned Dane,
> Drinke off this Potion: Is thy *Vnion* heere?
> Follow my Mother.[1]

---

[1] Bradley, who is seldom credited with any insight into the language of the plays, realised the full implications of this quibble. I have quoted the Folio. The Quarto printer was baffled by the word *union*. See *Hamlet*, ed. T. Parrott and H. Craig, p. 240.

VI

MACBETH

Whereas Coleridge could not recall a single pun or play on words in *Macbeth*, with the exception of the Porter's speeches which he thought to be an interpolation of the actors, the play's most recent editor discovers them in almost every scene.[1] Coleridge, of course, was thinking only of deliberate, witty wordplay. Although the play is not devoid of such puns in character, the ambiguities revealed by present-day commentators are rather Shakespeare's own puns, the ironic *double-entendres* we should expect in a tragedy of equivocation. At each turn of the action Shakespeare palters with us not merely in a double but in a treble sense; the irony is often negative as well as positive, since this is a play in which 'nothing is, but what is not'. Duncan, for example, bestows Cawdor's title on Macbeth with the words 'What he hath lost, Noble Macbeth hath wonne'; a statement that is true and untrue in ways unsuspected by the king. Cawdor's repentant death is to free him from the opprobrium of treachery which Macbeth is now to assume; on the other hand Cawdor does not lose that manliness which Macbeth, although he possessed it in the battle, relinquishes when he dares do more than may become a man and so 'is none'.

Time and again the play of verbal meanings reinforces such irony. It happens in the tragic anticipation of Macduff after the murder has been discovered:

> Malcolme, Banquo,
> As from your Graues rise vp, and walke like Sprights,
> To *countenance* this horror. (II.iii.85-7)

[1] The New Arden Shakespeare: *Macbeth*, ed. by Kenneth Muir. Many of the play's quibbles are discussed by the same writer in 'The Uncomic Pun', *Cambridge Journal*, III (1950), pp. 472-85. My own count for the play is 114 puns. Some of these are doubtful, but there are certainly a hundred.

Countenance here means, for Macduff, 'be in keeping with'. It also means for Shakespeare, and ultimately for us the hearers, 'give tacit consent to'. By a time-serving assent to Macbeth's election, Banquo puts himself in a position of danger and finally is murdered—only to walk as a ghost and confront his murderer. On re-readings of *Macbeth*, instances of wordplay such as this fall together with other aspects of the play's language into that pattern of ideas which contributes so much, though often at an unconscious level, to our excitement in the play's action.

1

A predominant element in this pattern is the theme of time— a theme which is hard to discuss since the most casual speculation about time can plunge us out of our depth in metaphysical deep waters. In discussing Shakespeare's use of the time theme in *Macbeth* I am using as a lifeline the main distinctions of meaning drawn by the *N.E.D.* They are not philosophical, but they represent the universally recognised distinctions which would have, and still have, meaning for Shakespeare's audience. The dictionary, then, gives us three main definitions: a space or extent of time; a point of time, a space of time treated without reference to its duration; and the first and most important of various general meanings, 'indefinite continuous duration'. The relation between the second and third of these meanings is paradoxical. If time is a continuum, it can be argued that there is no such thing as 'a time' but only the flux of events towards and away from a point without extension; we cannot step even once into the same stream. On the other hand, the reality of an action is not lessened or removed by its distancing in time: 'All time is eternally present.' In *Macbeth*, this contradiction between the fixed and the moving aspects of time is in some degree reconciled by the use of the word in the dictionary's first meaning and the supplementary meanings that derive from it. It is tempo, rhythm, measure, the fitness of the natural order—order, that is, seen as a recurrent succession of events, season after season, generation after generation; the revolution of the starry wheels under the law that preserves the stars from wrong. Fundamentally, it is a religious concept of time, in which the change of hour and season, the bow in the heavens, symbolises both the impermanence of things within time and their extra-temporal permanence. In the play it is associated with the powers of good—Duncan, Malcolm, Macduff—whereas the concept of time as the momentous event alone might be said to dominate the thoughts and actions of Lady Macbeth, and the concept of time as duration alone might be said to belong to Macbeth. The confrontation of these notions of time, the religious and the irreligious, is the play's major dramatic conflict. Lady Macbeth tells Macbeth to 'beguile the time', he bids her 'mock the time'; and, when Malcolm depicts himself as a second Macbeth, Macduff tells him that he may 'hoodwink' the time. In each phrase *time* means society, whose rhythm of times and seasons, being divinely appointed, cannot be mocked.

De Quincey's great essay on *Macbeth* presents the murder of Duncan as a parenthesis in time: 'In order that a new world may step in, this world must for a time disappear. The murderers, and the murder, must be insulated—cut off by an immeasurable gulf from the ordinary tide and succession of human affairs—locked up and sequestered in some deep recess; we must be made sensible that the world of ordinary life is suddenly arrested . . . time must be annihilated; relation to things without abolished; and all must pass self-withdrawn into a deep syncope and suspension of earthly passion.'[1] If *time* implies the fit social order, the hour of Duncan's murder and the interval between the crime and Macbeth's election to the throne are timeless; and during these hours in which Scotland is without a king a corresponding disorder in the heavens sets the elements at odds and turns day into night. The two murderers have mocked and beguiled time-as-order with their own distorted and partial concepts of time. For both the deed is a parenthesis, a timeless moment, though each apprehends this timelessness in a different way from the other.

Lady Macbeth contemplates the deed in a mood of clear-sighted exultation; time stands still for 'this Nights great

[1] *Collected Writings*, ed. Masson (1897), X, p. 393.

businesse'. Already she has proclaimed her mastery over the natural sequence of time in

> Thy Letters haue transported me beyond
> This ignorant present, and I feele now
> The future in the instant,   (I.v.57-9)

and in the triumph with which she sets her hand on the wheel of Duncan's days:

> O neuer,
> Shall Sunne that Morrow see.   (I.v.61-2)

It is one of the greater ironies of the play that the instant of Duncan's murder, which Lady Macbeth feels to be timelessly momentous, should in fact become timeless as it is perpetuated in the recesses of her mind. Time being the condition of human life, the moment out of time must have the nature of heaven or hell. That it can belong to either is suggested in Macbeth's words before the banquet:

> Better be with the dead,
> Whom we, to gayne our peace, haue sent to peace,
> Then on the torture of the Minde to lye
> In restlesse *extasie*,   (III.ii.19-22)

where *ecstasy* implies, not 'a heavenly rapture' but 'the state of being beside oneself with anxiety or fear'. When Lady Macbeth invokes the powers that 'Stop up th'accesse, and passage to Remorse', she creates a hell within the mind, and the sleep-walking scene shows that, by the end of the play, she is never out of it.

Macbeth also conceives the murder as a timeless act, but in the sense that it belongs to time seen as flux and duration, so that the fatal moment is anticipated and recalled but never recognised as the *now*. This way of regarding time allays his revulsion from the deed: 'Time, and the Houre, runs through the roughest Day'. It sets him safely upon the bank and shoal of time—the timeless moment in the river of successive events.[1] Even his last speech before the murder jumps over the deed itself in its sequence of ideas: 'I goe and it is done.' But once again time which may not be mocked takes its ironic revenge.

[1] See above, pp. 23-4

Lady Macbeth sees time as the great instant, and that instant persists traumatically in her mind. Macbeth sees it only as flux, and the flux of time brings the children of his victims to maturity and power so that they may avenge their fathers. Before Banquo is killed, Macbeth mocks the time by talk of their future meetings at the evening's banquet and the next day's Council. Time is in his power. He can shorten Banquo's days as easily as he has shortened Duncan's; after dismissing the thanes with the injunction that 'euery man be master of his time, Till seuen at Night', he calls in Banquo's assassins. But the next scene with Lady Macbeth shows him to be mastered by time, overpowered by fears lest his plans go astray and the succession pass from his line to Banquo's. Because murder has proved so easy, he may as easily be murdered before he has secured the succession to his own heirs.[1]

Several critics have shown that children are a *leitmotiv* of *Macbeth* and that the play abounds in contrasting images of barrenness and fertility.[2] Verbal ambiguities help to buttress the stress and counterstress of these themes. The heath which is *blasted* in a double sense—both barren and accursed—affords the right setting for the asexual witches who belong, in the play's pattern of ideas, with Lady Macbeth's readiness to dash her own child to death, with Macbeth's willingness to see nature's germens tumble altogether 'Euen till destruction sicken', with the avaricious farmer who hanged himself on the expectation of plenty, and with Malcolm's threat, in the disguise of a tyrant, to 'Poure the sweet Milke of Concord, into Hell'. On the other hand, the association of Duncan, Banquo and the English king

---

[1] The question of whether Macbeth had children or not is irrelevant, because even if he had them he has himself set a precedent for their being thrust from their inheritance. Macbeth's identification of himself with his victim in this scene ('Better be with the dead . . .') is sustained in an ambiguous phrase used by him when he and Lady Macbeth are alone after the banquet:

> Augures, and vnderstood Relations, haue
> By Maggot Pyes, & Choughes, & Rookes brought forth
> The secret'st man of Blood.

This last phrase, while it means the blood-guilty murderer, also suggests the blood-stained victim.

[2] See especially L. C. Knights: 'How many Children had Lady Macbeth?' in *Explorations* (1946); and Cleanth Brooks on 'The Naked Babe and the Cloak of Manliness', *The Well-Wrought Urn* (1949).

Edward with images of health and fertility is helped by such phrases as Duncan's

> My plenteous Ioyes,
> Wanton in *fulnesse*, seeke to hide themselues
> In drops of sorrow,   (I.iv.33-5)

where *fulness* has the suggestion of 'pregnancy' as well as its more general meaning of 'abundance'; and by the words of Lennox who is ready with the other thanes to shed his blood against tyranny: 'To dew the *Soueraigne* Flower, and drowne the Weeds'. *Sovereign*, by its double meaning of 'royal' and 'healing' recalls the curative powers of the holy Edward, the pattern of kings and the greatest possible contrast to the barren tyrant Macbeth.

Time had once seemed to befriend Macbeth, when its flow had carried him safely past the intolerable moment of Duncan's murder. Now this same movement, by its renewal of a broken social order, makes time Macbeth's greatest enemy. He first comes to feel the antagonism after his second encounter with the witches. As the vision of Banquo's progeny fades, messengers gallop past with the news that Macduff has fled to join Malcolm:

> Time thou anticipat'st my dread exploits:
> The flighty purpose neuer is o're-tooke
> Vnlesse the deed go with it. From this moment,
> The very *firstlings* of my heart shall be
> The *firstlings* of my hand.   (IV.i.144-8)

Firstlings can mean 'firstborn young' as well as 'the first results of anything, or first-fruits'. Macbeth has no children but acts of violence against the children of others. Meanwhile the young Malcolm, so seemingly helpless at the time of the murder, is strengthened by the quickening power of the English king and by the 'bloody babe', Macduff, and thus finds 'the time to friend' and 'the time of help'. When Macduff swears revenge on the murderer of his children, Malcolm cries 'This time goes manly'; and while 'tune' and 'time' were so similar as to be easily confused in Elizabethan handwriting, it seems a pity here to make the emendation to 'tune' and so lose the suggestion that time has brought the weak and oppressed to maturity and strength. Time now connotes only barrenness, sterility, 'dusty death' to Macbeth. On the other hand, natural abundance and the seasonal, renewing aspect of time are brought together in the wish of the anonymous Lord that

> we may againe
> Giue to our Tables meat, sleepe to our Nights
> (III.vi.33-4)

—a wish fulfilled when Malcolm and Macduff, who will do all things 'in measure, time and place' declare that 'the time is free'.

2

This time pattern of the play—the total view of time as Boethius's circle radiating from eternity, as the continual renewal of times and season which yet have permanence in their extra-temporal aspects, opposed to the partial views which see time only as point or line, crisis or continuum—is strengthened by Shakespeare's play upon the meanings of several keywords. The word *done*, for example, is associated, like appropriate music in a melodrama, with the entrances and exits of the two chief characters:

> If it were *done*, when 'tis *done*, then 'twer well,
> It were *done* quickly.   (I.vii.1-2)

There is, I suspect, much more to this than the meaning: 'If the murder were over and done with once it was committed, it ought to be done without delay.' Such a reading heightens the effect of compunction which Macbeth gives in this same speech as he contemplates the murder of his kinsman, king and guest. But as things turn out, Macbeth feels little remorse for the deed, once it is safely accomplished. If we reverse the ostensible meanings of *done*, we get 'If the deed were really performed once it was over and done with, it would be a good thing to do it without hesitation'; and this meaning, improbable at the moment of speaking, gains in probability as the play proceeds and Macbeth's victims are seen to live on, Banquo in his haunting as well as in his children, Duncan in the royal line which the usurper splits but cannot sever. The idea of resurrection is strong in such lines as Macbeth's

> Rebellious dead, rise never . . .   (IV.i.97)

136

and Menteith's

> Reuenges burne in them: for their deere causes
> Would to the bleeding, and the grim Alarme
> Excite the mortified man.   (V.ii.3-5)

Together with Lady Macbeth's 'He cannot come out on's graue', these passages give point to the echo, in 'If it were done . . .' of 'That thou doest, do quickly'. But Macbeth is no Judas to hang himself from remorse. The ambiguity of this rhythmically seesaw phrase is particularly subtle because it points to a reversal in the relationship of Macbeth and Lady Macbeth, once the deed is over. In order to quench the compunction she believes Macbeth to feel, and which the ostensible meaning of 'If it were done . . .' causes us to believe he also feels, Lady Macbeth deliberately suppresses her own remorse; but the secondary meaning of the phrase suggests that Macbeth is to harden into 'the deed's creature', since, provided the murder is successfully and completely performed, he is able to relegate it to the past.

This reversal, by which the remorseless Lady Macbeth comes to bear a weight of submerged guilt and the compunctious Macbeth comes to kill Macduff's children in unreflecting fury ('be it thoght & *done*'), is implicit in Lady Macbeth's attempt to comfort Macbeth before the banquet: 'What's *done*, is *done*.' The words may mean 'It's all over and past now, and so it can be put out of mind'; and in this sense they are shadowed by a negative irony. The murder is not over and past, but hauntingly present in her subconscious mind where it will later stir her to madness. She can also mean: 'You must resign yourself to the fact that you *are* a murderer; the crime is indubitably committed', and this in its turn carries a negative irony. Macbeth's reply: 'We haue scorch'd the Snake, not kill'd it' shows that for him the deed is not really accomplished until Banquo and his son and Duncan's are also dead. The same play of meanings recurs when the murdered Banquo takes Macbeth's seat at the banquet and Lady Macbeth, who cannot see the apparition, seeks to calm her husband with the words

> When all's *done*
> You looke but on a stoole.   (III.iv.67-8)

The phrase, usually equivalent to 'after all' and practically meaningless, is here charged with dramatic irony. What has been done, unknown to Lady Macbeth, is Banquo's murder; but the murderers' final words after the deed: 'Well let's away, and say how much is done', show that *all* is not done. Fleance has escaped, and hearing of his escape Macbeth exclaims:

> Then comes my Fit againe:
> I had else been *perfect*.   (III.iv.20)

To the play between two meanings of *perfect* here noticed by Dr Wilson—'completely satisfied' and 'whole and sound'[1]— we might add at least a nuance of the grammatical meaning (the perfect tense describes an action which is completed, that is, *done*) and certainly, as a negative irony, the biblical meaning of 'faultless'.[2] Finally there is Lady Macbeth's last use of *done*:

> To bed, to bed: there's knocking at the gate; Come, come, come, come, give me your hand: What's *done*, cannot be *undone*. To bed, to bed, to bed.   (V.i.72-6)

Terror and pity commingle to give this proverbial cliché its profoundly tragic effect. There is the terrible irony of the justicers above in the untruth of the statement; the murder can be undone, in the sense that the usurpation fails and that the wrong done to Duncan is in some degree righted with the accession of Malcolm; and this undoing begins with Macduff's knocking at the gate. The pathos of the words lies in their truth as they apply to Lady Macbeth herself. When she takes the hand that would 'the multitudinous seas incarnardine' she has already assumed a burden of guilt from which she will never again be free.

In Macbeth's first great soliloquy, wordplay upon the theme of time continues after the opening quibbling upon *done*:

> If th'Assassination
> Could *trammell* vp the *Consequence*, and catch
> With his *surcease*, *Successe* . . .

---

[1] New Cambridge edition, p. 181.

[2] I think there is another ironic pun in the banquet scene when Macbeth complains that the slain now rise
> With twenty mortall murthers on their *crownes*,
> And push us from our stooles.

When Banquo reappears—still 'blood-bolter'd'—in the witches' cavern, Macbeth cries: 'Thy Crowne do's seare mine Eye-bals.' Twenty mortal wounds cannot prevent Banquo's children succeeding to the crown and pushing Macbeth's line from the throne.

Consequence, besides meaning 'effect or result'—here Macbeth's seizure of the throne—suggests the meaningless sequence of tomorrow and tomorrow which is all the tyrant gains from his usurpation: T. S. Eliot's 'trailing Consequence of further days and hours'. Mr Empson also finds here the meaning 'a person of consequence', and there is some warrant for this in an earlier scene of the play.[1] At Macbeth's first meeting with the witches, Banquo warns him that

> The Instruments of Darknesse tell vs Truths,
> Winne vs with honest Trifles, to betray's
> In deepest *consequence*,   (I.iii.124-6)

where one meaning of the word is 'matter of importance'. This same earlier scene offers a pointer to the richness of *success* in Macbeth's soliloquy. The supernatural soliciting of the witches on the heath gives him

> earnest of *successe*
> Commencing in a Truth.   (I.iii.132-3)

Success could mean the bad as well as the good outcome of an action (the *N.E.D.* quotes Drayton: 'diuers unfortunat successes in warre'), and it had the further meaning of the succession of heirs. The witches, in giving earnest of succession to Banquo and not to Macbeth, have ensured that the outcome or success of Duncan's murder shall not be fortunately successful for Macbeth. So with the phrase 'and catch With his surcease, Successe': if *surcease* means, as it does in *Lucrece* (line 1766), 'decease', success as a fortunate outcome is possible for Macbeth; but if *surcease* has its legal meaning of the temporary stopping of a law-suit, the outcome for Macbeth is not going to be fortunate once this even-handed justice resumes its course in the succession of Malcolm to his father's authority.[2]

Trammel, in this passage, can mean 'suspend' and so suggest

[1] *Seven Types of Ambiguity*, pp. 49-50.
[2] In I.iii.120 Banquo's warnings to Macbeth begin
> That trusted home
> Might yet enkindle you vnto the Crowne.

The modern editors gloss *enkindle* as 'incite', a figurative use of the sense 'to set on fire'; but Coleridge thought the image was taken from the kindling, or breeding, of rabbits. Coming from Banquo, the words gain strong irony from this connotation, which fits well into the play's pattern of sterility-fertility images.

Lady Macbeth's attempt to arrest the natural sequence of life; or it can mean 'to net' or 'to hobble' and so foreshadow Macbeth's sense of being 'cabin'd, crib'd, confin'd' in the normal processes of time, that flux of events which now seems to befriend him, but is soon to prove his enemy. The witches' promise to Banquo that his children shall be kings becomes, for Macbeth,

> That great *Bond*,
> Which keepes me *pale*,　(III.ii.49-50)

where *bond* in the meaning of 'something that constricts' gives rise to a secondary sense, 'fenced in', for *pale*.[1] There is the same kind of interplay between the words in Macbeth's resolve to kill Macduff:

> But yet Ile make assurance: double sure,
> And take a *Bond* of Fate: thou shalt not liue,
> That I may tell *pale-hearted* Feare, it lies;
> And sleepe in spight of Thunder.　(IV.i.83-6)

There is 'a time to kill, and a time to heal; a time to break down, and a time to build up'. Time, which has brought to fruition the witches' promises for Macbeth must now, in its inescapable movement, bring also to fruition their prophecies regarding Banquo's children and Macduff. Another play on the legal and the common meanings of a word substantiates the same theme:

> *Macb.*　O, full of Scorpions is my Minde, deare Wife:
> 　　　　Thou know'st, that Banquo and his Fleans liues.
> *Lady.*　But in them, Nature's *Coppie's* not eterne.　(III.ii.36-8)

Nature's copyhold, the tenure of life at the will of the lord of the manor, is not unending for either Banquo or Fleance; in this respect Macbeth can master time by tearing to pieces Banquo's bond of life. But in time's natural, regenerative process, Banquo and Fleance are copied in their descendants; and that copy seems eternal to Macbeth as he watches the procession of kings who are to descend from Banquo: 'What will the Line stretch out to th' cracke of Doome?'

The same notion of life as tenure gives rise, at the end of the

---

[1] J. D. Wilson favours the emendation *pal'd*. See above, p. 38, for a discussion of the whole passage.

play, to Old Siward's stoical quibbling when he learns of his son's death:

> They say he parted well, and paid his *score*,
> And so God be with him.   (V.vii.81-2)

It was a brief reckoning of some twenty years, and his father sees it as honorably paid:

> Had I as many Sonnes, as I haue *haires*,
> I would not wish them to a fairer death.
>
> (77-8)

Young Siward's death represents the last blind attempt of Macbeth to render his enemies childless. It fails because Old Siward, in his impersonal role of a force of right and order, has many *heirs*: the children of Duncan and of Banquo, and the bloody babe, Macduff. Through them the natural order of succession, in which 'to everything there is a season' is restored to Scotland after the nightmare parenthesis of Macbeth's tyranny. The broken sleep of Macbeth and his wife is symbolic of their disruption of the normal sequence of life. 'You lacke the *season* of all Natures, sleepe', Lady Macbeth says after the banquet; the word implies not merely a preservative, but also the rhythmic, restorative variations of nature. Macbeth has deprived himself of 'great Natures second *Course*, Chiefe nourisher in Life's Feast'; and *course*, in the sense of 'ordered movement' ('the stars in their courses') connects by more than a poor paronomasia with a course as part of a meal. The fertility of the land and the health of the body natural or body politic are dependent alike on the recurrent rhythm of times and seasons. Macbeth suffers in his single state of man all the disorder he has brought upon the greater organism of the state.

3

A theme in *Macbeth* which is closely linked with that of time, and which is likewise built up largely through a play of meanings, is the theme of darkness. Light measures time; there is no time in the dark,[1] and before the parenthesis-in-time of

---

[1] Not until the clock strikes. In order for his deed to be out of time, Macbeth desires to be unheard as well as unseen:

> Thou sure and firme-set Earth
> Heare not my steps, which way they walke, for feare

Duncan's murder a menacing darkness is created in the edgy conversation of Banquo and Fleance as they cross the courtyard on their way to bed. Images of sight and blindness are a constituent part of this darkness theme, and they reveal, as vividly as the time theme, a fundamental difference between Macbeth and Lady Macbeth. Whereas both husband and wife seek to conceal their act from the eyes of men and heaven ('Starres hide your fires'—'Come thick Night'), Macbeth performs blindly an act that Lady Macbeth is able to contemplate clear-sightedly. She bids him 'Onely looke vp cleare'; but he desires the action to be lost in the dark as the moment of its perpetration is lost in the sequence of time. He must compel his eye to wink at his hand in doing the deed, and cannot return to the sight of the murdered Duncan once he has left the chamber. The blood which evokes his horrifying cry—'What Hands are here? hah: they pluck out mine Eyes', is to Lady Macbeth merely 'this filthie Witnesse' which may give away their complicity to others. The same decisive clarity shows itself in her grim and lucid puns, which are the voluntary wordplay of a totally self-possessed mind:

> He that's comming,
> Must be prouided for: and you shall put
> This Nights great Businesse into my *dispatch*;
>
> (I.v.67-69)
>
> But screw your courage to the *sticking place*;
>
> (I.vii.60-1)
>
> Ile guild the Faces of the Groomes withall,
> For it must seeme their *Guilt*.
>
> (II.ii.57-8)

As Cleanth Brooks has shown, this last pun is deeply expressive; Lady Macbeth sees guilt as something that can be washed off or

> Thy very stones prate of my where-about,
> And take the present horror from the time,
> Which now sutes with it.   (II.i.56-60)

The meaning of this shifts according to the sense of *horror* and the grammatical role of *take*. *Take* can be an imperative—'Take away my fear', or a subjunctive like 'prate'—'for fear lest the stones, by their sound, break this horrible silence which accords so well with the deed'. If *horror* signifies the murder itself, the line can mean that Macbeth is afraid lest the noise he makes causes him to be detected and prevented from killing Duncan. Nothing less than all three meanings together will convey the turmoil of Macbeth's mind.

painted on.[1] The crime's real horror appears to her as a mere image:

> the sleeping, and the dead,
> Are but as Pictures: 'tis the Eye of Child-hood,
> That feares a painted Deuill,   (II.ii.54-6)

and in the same fashion she dismisses Banquo's ghost, real to Macbeth and the audience although invisible to her, as the 'very painting' of his fear. To Macbeth, on the other hand, mere images such as those that form when the witches drag to the surface his thoughts of murder, have a seemingly tangible reality. The 'horrid Image' which takes shape after Ross has hailed him thane of Cawdor is more real and fearful to him than the 'Strange Images of death' he had himself made in the battle. Whereas Lady Macbeth's *double-entendres* clinch her arguments by their neat riveting of two distinct meanings (and *clinch* was one seventeenth-century name for a pun), Macbeth's word-play is exploratory and indicates his gropings in the chimera-haunted darkness of his mind. In that the poetic process is often a similar exploration, Macbeth is quite as 'imaginative' as Bradley maintained. I have already suggested that the dynamic of Macbeth's invocation 'Come, seeling Night' is in the separative force of the different meanings in such words as 'seeling', 'deed', 'bond' and 'pale'.[2] The soliloquy 'If it were done . . .' works by the same process. The excited association of images through wordplay in the opening lines is checked by a moment of reasoned reflection as Macbeth reviews the arguments against the murder:

> Hee's heere in double trust;
> First, as I am his Kinsman, and his Subiect,
> Strong both against the Deed; Then, as his Host,
> Who should against his Murtherer shut the doore,
> Not *beare* the knife my selfe.

Beare can be either 'bare' or 'bear'; and the idea of exposure, to his own sight as well as to that of others, gives rise to a renewed rhythmic excitement and to the complex images of the naked babe and the cherubim:

> Besides, this Duncane
> Hath borne his Faculties so meeke; hath bin

---

[1] *Op. cit.*, p. 40.   [2] See above, pp. 38-9

So cleere in his great Office, that his Vertues
Will pleade like Angels, Trumpet-tongu'd against
The deepe damnation of his taking off:
And Pitty, like a naked New-borne-Babe,
Striding the *blast*, or Heauens Cherubin, hors'd
Vpon the *sightlesse* Curriors of the Ayre,
Shall *blow* the horrid deed in euery eye,
That teares shall drowne the winde. I haue no Spurre
To pricke the sides of my intent, but onely
Vaulting Ambition, which ore-leapes it selfe,
And falles on th' other.

Again the wordplay helps the imagery; *blast* connects 'trumpet-tongued' with the couriers of the air ('He rode upon the Cherubyns and did flye; he came flyenge with the winges of the wynde'), and *blow*, by suggesting a sorrow that is both active and passive, that can trumpet the name of the murderer abroad as well as make every eye weep for his victim, sustains the paradox of the strong weakling. The final image from horsemanship is so vivid that it makes possible a kind of long-distance pun in Macbeth's words after the murder:

> Renowne and *Grace* is dead,
> The Wine of Life is drawne, and the meere Lees
> Is left this *Vault*, to brag of. (II.iii.111-13)

In the first instance this means: 'Now that the famous and gracious Duncan is dead, this earth over-arched by the heavens is as an empty wine-cellar that cannot boast of containing anything better than dregs.' But for us, the audience, it also means: 'I have lost my reputation and Heaven has withdrawn its grace from me. The best of my life is over, and I am left, the bitter dregs of my former self, able to boast of nothing except the ambitious murder of my king.' Most interesting of all the ambiguities in the soliloquy is *sightless*. The dominant meaning would seem to be that the couriers of the air, the winds, are invisible. Blake, however, took the word in another Shakespearean sense when he drew them as blind. The contradiction suggests Macbeth's own behaviour, closing his eyes to a deed he dare not contemplate and yet which he knows to be visible to the pity of Heaven.

The figure of Pity soon fades from Macbeth's imagination—

sooner, indeed, than Lady Macbeth anticipates. 'For her there is no moral order' Cleanth Brooks writes in explanation of the *gilt-guilt* pun. But Lady Macbeth acknowledges the fact of a moral order when she summons the powers of darkness to 'Stop up th'accesse, and passage to Remorse.' The moral order exists for her, but it is kept at distance by an act of the will, only to return during sleep when the will is in abeyance. The moral blindness of Macbeth comes involuntarily upon him as a result of the murder; and the success with which Lady Macbeth has taught him bloody instructions shows itself when he begins to imitate her wordplay. The horror of 'sticking-place' which presents Macbeth, his nerves as taut as lute-strings, stabbing the sleeping king, is rekindled by 'Our feares in Banquo *sticke* deepe', preparing us for the twenty trenched gashes of the second murder and for Macbeth's callous equivocation: 'But Banquo's *safe*?' Once again a reversal of Macbeth's and Lady Macbeth's experience has been achieved by the turning wheel of an ironic fate. Lady Macbeth, for whom the real murder seemed a mere picture, comes to accept the images of nightmare as actuality. She begins in the light, acting with decision and clarity, knowing her own mind as Macbeth never knows his; she ends in the dark, open-eyed and carrying a light, but seeing only Duncan's blood on her hands. Macbeth begins in the dark:

> To know my deed,
> 'Twere best not know my selfe.   (II.ii.74)

He ends in the light, forced into the open by the powers of order whose lighting of the play's darkness begins at 'The Night is long, that neuer findes the Day'; forced also by the bitterness of experience to see life as a candle that lights folly its way into the dark.

The wordplay of *Macbeth*, less obvious than that of other plays, is some of the most subtle Shakespeare has given us. It welds the themes of the play together into the imaginative unity of a great dramatic poem. At the same time it preserves the play's theatrical vigour by contributing to the interplay of characters as fully realised as any in the major group of Shakespeare's tragedies.

VII

THE WINTER'S TALE

1

At this late hour, it would be a work of supererogation to defend the last plays of Shakespeare against the charges of dullness and incompetence which were once frequent in criticism. On a superficial level, there is little to distinguish such as play as *The Winter's Tale* from the fashionable romances of Beaumont and Fletcher; but as recent writers have demonstrated,[1] Shakespeare's poetry in these last plays is too intense to be read superficially. Each image, each turn of phrase, each play upon a word's meanings, compels us to feel that Shakespeare's total statement adds up to much more than the fairy-tale events of the plot. Yet in the theatre the impetus of the action itself leaves us no time to ponder this deeper significance which remains at or very near the unconscious level, and so inseparable from our theatrical excitement and wonder at Leontes' jealousy, Perdita's preservation, and the return to life of Hermione.

Shakespeare packs meaning into *The Winter's Tale* in a way that might be instanced by the opening words of the second scene. Polixenes, the visiting king, is anxious to get home:

> Nine Changes of the Watry-Starre hath been
> The Shepheards Note, since we haue left our Throne
> Without a Burthen.

After the naturalistic prose dialogue with which the play began, this orotund phrase achieves one of those swift changes in the

---

[1] Especially S. L. Bethell, *The Winter's Tale, a Study* (1947); G. Wilson Knight, *The Crown of Life* (1947); F. R. Leavis, 'The Criticism of Shakespeare's Late Plays' in *Scrutiny* X; E. M. W. Tillyard, *Shakespeare's Last Plays* (1938); and D. A. Traversi, *Shakespeare: The Last Phase* (1955).

pressure of realism—here from contemporary Court life to the world of the Player King—which is typical of the dramatic climate of these last plays. But the image accomplishes much more than that. The moon's nine changes imply the themes of pregnancy (helped, perhaps, by 'Burthen'), of sudden changes of fortune, and of madness, which are all to become explicit in the course of the same scene. The whole image is the first of many taken from country things and the pastoral life, which persist throughout the Sicilian scenes of the play and so help to bridge the 'great gap' of time and place over which we pass later to the shepherd kingdom of Bohemia. And the leading theme of these scenes in Bohemia, the summer harmony of heaven and earth, is prepared here by mention of the 'watery star' that draws the tides.

For instances of wordplay which, in their economy, match these uses of imagery, we may go back to the opening dialogue between Camillo and Archidamus. Although there are not very many puns in *The Winter's Tale*, the few that are used generate a superb energy. This opening dialogue, for instance, seems no more than the explanatory chat between two minor characters which is part of the competent dramatist's stock-in-trade; but some enquiry into its play of meanings shows it to be much more than this. 'If you shall chance (Camillo)', Archidamus begins, 'to visit Bohemia, on the like occasion whereon my seruices are now on-foot, you shall see (as I haue said) great *difference* betwixt our *Bohemia* and your *Sicilia*.' This *difference* we shall soon discover to be 'contention' as well as 'dissimil- arity'; for *Bohemia* and *Sicily* stand eponymously for the kings as well as the kingdoms—as, after a brief exchange of civilities, Camillo's words indicate:

> *Sicilia* cannot shew himselfe ouer-kind to *Bohemia*: They were *trayn'd* together in their Child-hoods; and there rooted betwixt them then such a affection, which cannot chuse but *braunch* now.
>
> (I.i.23-8)

Trained, used of fruit trees as well as of the education of children, introduces an image of two plants united in such a way as to propagate new growth, and this anticipates the talk in

Act IV of grafting a noble scion upon the wildest stock, which is symbolic both of the union of court and country in Perdita's upbringing as a Shepherd's daughter and of the reunion of the two kings through the marriage of Perdita and Florizel. But *branch*, besides meaning 'throw out new shoots from the family tree', has the sense of 'divide'; and 'Sicilia cannot show himself over-kind' is ambiguous. On the one hand the undertones of the scene prepare us for the fertility legend of a child healing an old man and so bringing prosperity to the land; on the other hand, the secondary meanings of *difference* and *branch*, together with Camillo's ominous insistence upon Mamillius's 'promise', prepare us for the estrangement of the kings and the death of Mamillius which must intervene before a child, Perdita, 'Physicks the Subject, makes old hearts fresh'.

Some of the most richly ambiguous wordplay in all Shakespeare occurs at the beginning of this estrangement, in Leontes' violent seizure of jealousy against Polixenes. It is possible, of course, to read long-standing suspicion into all Leontes' speeches to Polixenes and Hermione, from the first appearance of the three characters.[1] But this impairs the dramatic contrast between the happiness and harmony of the three characters when Polixenes has agreed to stay, and Leontes' subsequent outburst of passion:

> Too hot, too hot:
> To mingle friendship farre, is mingling bloods.
> I haue Tremor Cordis on me: my heart daunces,
> But not for ioy; not ioy.   (I.ii.109-12)

Unlike the Age of the Enlightenment, with its demand for logically clear motivation of character, the pre-Locke and the post-Freud epochs share an acceptance of the seemingly incalculable in human behaviour. The Elizabethans might have put Leontes' outburst down to demonic possession; we should call it a libidinous invasion. The effect in either case is the same—a sudden outburst of normally suppressed feelings,

[1] This was done by John Gielgud in his 1951 production at the Phoenix Theatre, London; and there is some warrant for it in Greene's *Pandosto*, from which Shakespeare took the story. But Greene also speaks of a certain melancholy passion *entering* the king's mind.

which struggle for their release in savage wordplay. Leontes'
puns erupt like steam forcing up a saucepan lid, and by the end
of some hundred lines he has fairly boiled over with 'foul
imaginings'. There are the conscious puns which release his
obscene and aggressive tendencies in

> We must be *neat*; not *neat*, but *cleanly*, Captaine:
> And yet the Steere, the Heyfer, and the Calfe,
> Are all call'd *Neat*, (I.ii.124-6)

and in—

> Let what is *deare* in Sicily, be *cheape*:
> Next to thy selfe, and my young Rouer, he's
> *Apparant* to my heart, (175-7)

where *apparent* means 'seen-through, obvious' as well as 'heir-
apparent'. There are unconscious puns on words which remain
unspoken: *die*, for example, in 'and then to sigh, as 'twere The
Mort o'th'*Deere*' and perhaps *stews* in 'his Pond fish'd by his
next Neighbor'. And there are the innuendoes which Leontes
reads into Camillo's innocent use of such words as *business*
(216) and *satisfy* (232). At one point this kind of wordplay
becomes threefold, in that it reveals Shakespeare's intentions as
well as Leontes' disturbance of mind:

> Goe *play* (Boy) *play*: thy Mother *playes*, and I
> *Play* too; but so *disgrac'd* a part, whose *issue*
> Will hisse me to my Graue. (187-9)

Only the first *play* is used in a single sense. We might paraphrase Leontes' *double-entendres* thus: 'Go and amuse yourself;
your mother is also pretending to play by acting the kind
hostess, but I know that she is a real daughter of the game and
up to another sport which makes me act the contemptible role
of the deceived husband. So for the moment I'm playing her
like a fish ("I am angling now") by giving her line.' This
ironic wordplay of Leontes is sustained through *disgraced*,
meaning both 'ungraceful' and 'shameful', and *issue* meaning
'exit', 'result' and perhaps also 'Polixenes' bastard child that
Hermione now carries'. But *play*, *disgraced* and *issue* have other
functions besides that of rendering Leontes' paroxysm true to

life. Shakespeare counters each of Leontes' puns by further meanings which relate the word to the larger context of the play's thought and action. The meaning 'make-believe' is added in this way to all the senses of *play*. Leontes is play-acting in his outburst; it is characteristic of such obsessions as his that the sufferer is deluded yet half knows he is under a delusion— as when we know we are in a nightmare but cannot wake from it. Only the make-believe of Hermione, in playing at being a statue, and the make-believe of Perdita in playing the part of a shepherd's daughter, can restore Leontes to a sane discrimination between illusion and reality. *Disgraced* also has further meanings for the play as a whole: Leontes is without the grace of Heaven in sinning against Hermione; but because the irony of wordplay has a negative as well as a positive force, the word also foreshadows Hermione's symbolic role of Heavenly Grace which never deserts Leontes. *Issue* can, positively, mean Mamillius, whose death drives Leontes to a mortified existence; or it can be Leontes' 'action' (a meaning peculiar to Shakespeare)[1] in defying the oracle and so driving Mamillius to *his* grave. It can also mean the legal issue of Hermione's trial. Perhaps its strongest ironic meaning is 'child', taken negatively; Perdita will, in fact, restore him to life. Perdita is preserved from a death of exposure, Leontes is reclaimed from his life-in-death of grief, and Hermione is called upon to bestow to death her numbness, and all this is in accordance with the oracle of Apollo since 'to the Lord God belong the issues of death'.

2

We can quote the Geneva Bible with no sense of incongruity. The presiding deity of the play may be Apollo, but the Christian scheme of redemption is a leading element, though not by any means the only element, in its pattern of ideas. *Grace*, with *gracious* a keyword of the play, is frequently used in its theological sense of 'the divine influence which operates in men to

---

[1] As in *Julius Cæsar*, III.i.294: Antony calls Caesar's murder 'The cruell issue of these bloody men'; and *Cymbeline*, II.i.53: 'You are a Foole graunted, therefore your Issues being foolish do not derogate'—with a pun on the sense of 'offspring'.

regenerate and sanctify' (*N.E.D.* II.6b). As Everyman, Humanity, Leontes is able to recall a primeval innocence when he was 'Boy eternal':

> We were as twyn'd Lambs, that did frisk i'th'Sun,
> And bleat the one at th'other: what we chang'd,
> Was Innocence, for Innocence: we knew not
> The Doctrine of ill-doing, nor dream'd
> That any did: Had we pursu'd that life,
> And our weake Spirits ne're been higher rear'd
> With stronger blood, we should haue answer'd Heauen
> Boldly, not guilty; the Imposition clear'd,
> Hereditarie ours.   (I.ii.67-75)

In the dialogue which follows, the word *grace* is used three times by Hermione, the implication being that she acts the role of regenerative grace to Leontes now he has exchanged Innocence for Experience. But immediately there follows Leontes' rejection of this grace in his outburst against Hermione. 'You'le be found, Be you beneath the Sky' is his threat to Hermione and Polixenes; the words are strong dramatic irony, since it is Leontes himself who is sinning in the sight of Heaven, the single Eye of Apollo made actual to us by the sight images of Leontes' talk with Camillo in the first act—'your eye-glasse Is thicker then a Cuckolds Horne' (I.ii.268); 'a Vision so apparant' (270); 'to haue nor Eyes' (275); 'and all Eyes Blind with the Pin and Web, but theirs' (290); 'Canst with thine eyes at once see good and euill' (303); 'Seruants true about me, that bare eyes' (309); 'who may'st see Plainely, as Heauen sees Earth, and Earth sees Heauen' (314). The small but vitally important scene between Diomenes and Cleon, as they return from Delphos at the beginning of Act III, stresses this awesome aspect of the Destroyer Apollo, whose oracle is 'kin to Ioues Thunder'; and their hope that the *issue* of their visit will be *gracious* is not immediately fulfilled. Apollo keeps jealous guard over the fortunes of the gracious Hermione, and her belief that 'Powres Diuine Behold our humane Actions' is vindicated when, his oracle defied, Apollo at once smites Leontes with the death of Mamillius: 'Apollo's angry, and the Heauens themselues Doe strike at my Iniustice.'

Leontes's change of heart, from a proud defiance of the God

to guilt, despair and finally a sober repentance, is marked by two instances of wordplay. At the beginning of the trial scene he announces that justice shall have 'due course, Euen to the Guilt, or the *Purgation*'. In the legal sense, human justice will proceed to find Hermione guilty or give her the chance 'of clearing [her] self from the accusation or suspicion of crime and guilt'; in the theological sense, Apollo's justice will establish Leontes' guilt and will also purify him from it by the repentance vowed at the end of the scene:

> once a day, Ile visit
> The Chappell where they lye, and teares shed there
> Shall be my *recreation*.

Recreation and *re-creation*: the pun is a promise that Leontes is to become 'man new made' at the end of the play, for Apollo offers him grace in the sense of time for amendment (*N.E.D.*II 7) and also hope for the eventual grace of pardon (*N.E.D.*II 8). The King takes to himself the words of Hermione:

> I must be patient, till the Heauens looke
> With an aspect more fauorable,   (II.i.105-6)

and her withdrawal symbolises Everyman's patient hope in the return of grace. In the major tragedies of Shakespeare, patience had been a stoical virtue, the capacity to endure. Here it is a Christian virtue, the ability to possess one's soul in patience, which is rewarded when Hermione reappears literally as Patience on a monument, 'smiling' (in the words of *Pericles*) 'extremity out of act'.

Meanwhile Perdita has 'grown in grace'; as with Tuesday's child, the word has a theological as well as a physical meaning. At the sheep-shearing feast, Leontes' grace of repentance and Hermione's grace of patient forgiveness are kept in mind by Perdita's graceful presentation of flowers to the disguised Polixenes and Camillo:

> Reuerend Sirs,
> For you, there's Rosemary, and *Rue*, these keepe
> Seeming, and sauour all the Winter long:
> *Grace*, and Remembrance be to you both,
> And welcome to our Shearing.   (IV.iii.73-7)

The theological language of the play's first part is revived and intensified when the action returns to Sicily at the beginning of Act V. The restoration of both the wife and the daughter is spoken of as a regeneration for Leontes. 'Now blesse thy selfe:' the old shepherd had said at the finding of Perdita, 'thou met'st with things dying, I with things new borne'; and the theme is repeated when one courtier tells another how Leontes was re-united with Camillo: 'they look'd as they had heard of a World ransom'd, or one destroyed'. The ritual-like solemnity of the last scene completes this regeneration. 'It is requir'd', commands Paulina, 'You doe awake your Faith'; and to music such as accompanied the awakening of Lear and Pericles, Faith, in the person of Hermione, steps off her plinth into Leontes' arms:

> You Gods looke downe,
> And from your sacred Viols poure your graces
> Vpon my daughters head.   (V.iii.121-3)

3

So *The Winter's Tale* is a morality play; but its morality is wider, wiser and more humane than that of a Puritan inner drama of sin, guilt and contrition. Something is omitted in the attempt made here to allegorise the play. We have had to leave out the sunburnt mirth of the scenes in Bohemia, the Clown, Mopsa, and the rogue Autolycus who made such an impression on Simon Forman when he saw the play in 1611. Worse still, Perdita is really unnecessary if we read *The Winter's Tale* as a kind of *Grace Abounding*, and we are forced to ask why Shakespeare could not have symbolised the spiritual health of the lapsed and forgiven soul by a single figure like Dante's Beatrice or Blake's Jerusalem.

A clue to the answer may perhaps be found if we return to Leontes' outburst in Act I. After 'Goe play (Boy) play', Leontes abandons the ordinary sense of 'to sport or frolic' for bitterly ironic meanings; and in this wordplay, and the act of dismissing Mamillius, is revealed Leontes' inability to keep himself young, to become as a child again. Polixenes understands the value of play, and Florizel's 'varying child-nesse' keeps him from a spiritual winter. Mamillius also has the power to make old hearts fresh; the sight of him can take twenty-three years off his father's life, and he has a *welkin* eye—the adjective suggesting something providential and life-giving, and not merely 'clear and blue like the sky'. In spite of this, Leontes cannot recapture the non-moral vision of childhood, the state of the 'Boy eternal' who had not as yet the knowledge of good and evil. At the beginning of the last act, Cleomines pleads with Leontes to forgive himself; but this is just what Leontes cannot do until Perdita's return. For if Hermione represents the grace of heaven towards Leontes, Perdita stands for his self-forgiveness, for his recapture of the child's non-moral acceptance of things as they are in Nature. In this way, Perdita plays a role of Nature complementary to Hermione's role of Grace. This moral intransigence in Leontes may have very deep roots. J. I. M. Stewart hints at the transference, in the king's outburst of delusional jealousy, of his guilt at an adolescent relationship with Polixenes for which he cannot forgive himself.[1] Whatever the cause of his fury, his bawdy use of *play* in 'thy Mother playes' suggests the moral rigidity born of a moral uncertainty; he cannot see Hermione's real need to play, to the extent perhaps of a harmless flirtation with Polixenes. So a tension is established between two forms of *play*: play as sport, a holiday freedom, and play as Leontes' imprisoning delusion that Hermione is unfaithful to him. Unable to play in the sense of refreshing himself from the non-moral and instinctive life of childhood, Leontes begins to play in the sense of constructing an intensely moral drama in which he enacts the role of the deceived husband. In the opening scene of Act II, these two forms of play, the natural and the unnatural, are literally juxtaposed. On one side of the stage, Mamillius at play produces make-believe shudders with his ghost story; on the other, Leontes' delusion—'I have drunke, and seene the spider'—communicates a real horror to the audience who are to see him, in the grip of his involuntary make-believe, turn Mamillius's winter's tale into earnest. 'What is this? Sport?' Hermione asks as Mamillius is snatched from her; and once again Leontes perverts the meaning of the most innocent word:

[1] J. I. M. Stewart, *Character and Motive in Shakespeare* (1948), pp. 30-7.

> Away with him, and let her sport her selfe
> With that shee's big with, for 'tis Polixenes
> Ha's made thee swell thus. (II.i.59)

The contrast between these two kinds of play is kept up in Leontes' insistence that his delusion is fact:

> No: if I mistake
> In those Foundations which I build vpon,
> The Centre is not bigge enough to beare
> A Schoole-Boyes Top.[1] (II.i.99-102)

So deluded, he is beyond the reach of reason as it is voiced in the well-ordered rhetoric of Camillo or that of Hermione in her formal self-defence at the trial. Hermione is forced to admit that she and Leontes move in different worlds:

> You speake a Language that I vnderstand not:
> My Life stands in the leuell of your Dreames,
> Which Ile lay downe. (III.ii.81-3)

With much more irony than he intends, Leontes replies: 'Your Actions are my Dreames.' Nothing can in fact destroy his confusion of nightmare and reality except the real-life disaster of Mamillius's death.

For two and a half acts of the play the audience has shared an overcharged moral atmosphere, as it has witnessed Leontes' protest against his supposedly impaired honour, shared Paulina's moral indignation at Leontes' treatment of Hermione, and experienced with the whole Court a sense of heavenly retribution in the death of Mamillius. Now in the ensuing few scenes, this tension is relaxed and we are transported into a world on holiday. By its remoteness from the real Hermione of the trial scene, Antigonus's vision of Hermione begins the distancing of Sicily and Sicilian attitudes; and the shift from a courtly to a

---

[1] This is, I think, echoed in *Comus* when the Elder Brother declares that 'evil on it self shall back recoyl. . . .'
> if this fail,
> The pillar'd firmament is rott'nness
> And earths base built on stubble.

Comus has in common with Shakespeare's last plays more than the family likeness of a pastoral. It has been suggested by J. E. Crofts that Sabrina's role in the masque is very much that of a nature spirit such as Perdita. The Lady remains frozen in a Puritanical disapproval until the nymph releases her.

country outlook starts with the old shepherd's grumbles about the hunt and the coarse kindness with which he dismisses Perdita's begetting as 'behinde-doore worke: they were warmer that got this, then the poore Thing is heere'. There is a matter-of-fact acceptance of Nature as it is in the Clown's account of the shipwreck and of Antigonus's encounter with the bear. If his vivid descriptions of both seem callous, they are in fact only honest; hogsheads have more reality for him than have Sicilian courtiers, and he sees Antigonus's fate from the bear's point of view. The creature must have its dinner, and 'they are neuer *curst* but when they are hungry'; his use of the word to imply 'fierce' without any moral nuance contrasts with Leontes' use of it when in the grip of his delusion:

> How blest am I
> In my iust Censure? in my true Opinion?
> Alack, for lesser knowledge, how *accurs'd*
> In being so blest?   (II.i.35-8)

In *King Lear* a vision of Nature's cruelty, of man as one of the most savage beasts of prey, was opposed to the traditional notion of Nature as harmony, fecundity and order. In *The Winter's Tale*, however, Nature is neither morally good nor bad; a bear's appetite and a waiting-gentlewoman's lapse are accepted as the way of the world. Animal images are used by Leontes, in the first part of the play, with all the revulsion of Othello's 'goats and monkeys!' but Antigonus's stud language shows up, by a kind of grotesque parody, the folly of thus regarding everything in Nature as subject to moral judgment; and the scenes in Bohemia restore the child's or the peasant's freedom from morbid preoccupations about good and evil. The wordplay reveals the same change of attitude. *Blood*, for example, when used in the first part of the play, often carries a connotation of 'lust'—its primary meaning in a play like *Othello*. Now, in Autolycus's song about 'the red blood raigns in the winters pale', it represents a passion as natural and inevitable as the sap that rises in spring, to be accepted as philosophically as the old shepherd endures the ways of 'these boylde-braines of nineteene, and two and twenty'. For all his classical name, Autolycus is an English coney-catcher, and his daffodil and doxy belong less to the classical Arcadia[1] than to Herrick's Devonshire, where Christianity has absorbed much of an older cult, and if there is a Puritan he too sings psalms to hornpipes. According to Blake's paradox, the return of spiritual vision by which what now seemed finite and corrupt would appear infinite and holy was to be accomplished by 'an improvement of sensual enjoyment'; and such enjoyment is felt throughout the scenes in Bohemia. The sensuous blend of the colourful, the fragrant, the sweet and the spicy in the Clown's shopping list contrasts sharply with the painful sensibility of some images in the first part of the play—for instance, Leontes' rebuke to Antigonus:

> Cease, no more:
> You smell this businesse with a sence as *cold*
> As is a dead-mans nose,   (II.i.149-51)

where the wordplay, by suggesting the touch of death, achieves a *frisson* worthy of a winter's tale.

By the time Autolycus, who has overheard the Clown's list, has caught this particular coney in a travesty of the Good Samaritan story, the holiday mood is complete.[2] Like Florizel, we

> Apprehend
> Nothing but iollity: the Goddes themselues
> (Humbling their Deities to loue) haue taken
> The shapes of Beasts vpon them. Iupiter,
> Became a Bull, and bellow'd: the green Neptune
> A Ram, and bleated: and the Fire-roab'd-God
> Golden Apollo, a poore humble Swaine,
> As I seeme now.   (IV.iii.24-31)

These lines, based on a section of Greene's *Pandosto* which Shakespeare did not utilise in any other way, have a particular aptness to the holiday mood of this feast. Even the Gods are at

---

[1] Shakespeare may have changed round the Sicily and Bohemia of his source in order to avoid the literary associations of Sicilian shepherds.

[2] S. L. Bethell, in *The Winter's Tale, a Study*, discusses very fully the fade-out of Sicilian attitudes. The Biblical parallel, pointed out by G. Wilson Knight (*The Crown of Life*, p. 101) is given support by Autolycus's recall of how he once compassed a motion (that is, staged a puppet show) of the Prodigal Son.

play. Jupiter and Neptune become the horned animals in which Leontes saw only the symbol of human bestiality and cuckoldry, and their bellowing and bleating evoke the laughter which is lacking in Leontes, who cannot play. Greene's phrase: 'Neptune became a ram, Jupiter a Bull, Apollo a shepherd' may have recalled to Shakespeare the story told in the second book of the *Metamorphoses* of Apollo's love for the nymph Chione, whom in jealousy he slew with his dart, but whose child he reared to be the lifegiving Aesculapius; a parallel to his dual role of destroyer and preserver in *The Winter's Tale*. Apollo's metamorphosis into the shepherd 'humbling his Deity to love' is not incompatible with the presentation of Apollo as the supreme and just God in the first part of the play; it suggests just such a union of Heaven and earth as is implied by Milton's

> Or if Vertue feeble were,
> Heav'n it self would stoop to her.

But in these scenes of the play the reconciliation of heaven and earth is not theological but natural, the fructification of nature by the sun that shines alike upon the good and the evil. In the scenes of sixteen years before, heaven had been at destructive variance with earth in the 'dangerous vnsafe Lunes I' th' King', in Apollo's thunderbolt, and in the storm's conflict of sea and sky. Now the imagery stresses their harmony:

> for neuer gaz'd the Moone
> Vpon the water, as hee'l stand and reade
> As 'twere my daughters eyes. (IV.iii.172-4)

And in proof of his constancy, Florizel protests that not

> for all the Sun sees, or
> The close earth wombes, or the profound seas, hides
> In vnknowne fadomes, will I breake my oath
> To this my faire belou'd. (IV.iii.502-5)

The image persists after the lovers' voyage to Sicily. Perdita seems to Leontes at his first sight of her

> the most peereless peece of Earth, I thinke,
> That ere the Sunne shone bright on, (V.i.94-5)

and he tells how he

> lost a couple, that 'twixt Heauen and Earth
> Might thus haue stood, begetting wonder, as
> You (gracious Couple) doe,   (V.i.132-4)

where both the natural and the spiritual union are implied in
'begetting' and 'gracious'. This awareness of the bridal of the
earth and sky lends irony to Florizel's bitter assertion (V.i.206)
that the stars will kiss the valleys before he and Perdita will be
able to marry. The stars do kiss the valleys through those
heavenly influences in which most Jacobeans firmly believed;
heaven is matched with earth in the life of growth, in the
Bohemian shepherds' acceptance of nature's ways, of which
Perdita is the symbol.

For Perdita, dressed as the queen of the feast, and acting the
part of hostess to her father's guests, represents the natural
rightness of play, the renewing power of youth which Leontes
once had, and lost, in Mamillius. In her presentation of flowers,
time runs back to fetch the age of gold, from winter herbs to
August's carnations and striped gillyflowers, to the June
marigold that goes to bed with the sun (another symbol of the
union of heaven and earth), and so back to the spring flowers
she would give Florizel. The great flower passage is full of
what Herrick calls a 'cleanly wantonness': the violets are as
sweet as the breath of Venus, the primroses lovesick, the
oxslip inviting, and the daffodils *take* the air in a triple sense—
enchant, seize, and come out for exercise and pleasure—which
suggests all the tentative and yet bold grace of the flower.
The daffodil flings itself on the winds of March with that en-
chanting blend of abandon and modesty that is found in Perdita's
wish to strew Florizel with these flowers

> like a banke, for Loue to lye, and *play* on:
> Not like a Coarse: or if: not to be buried
> But quicke, and in mine armes. Come, take your flours,
> Me thinkes I *play* as I haue seene them do
> In Whitson-Pastorals: Sure this Robe of mine
> Do's change my disposition.   (IV.iii.130-5)

The first *play* here has the same connotation as 'thy Mother

playes', but it is used with an innocent sexuality which represents that acceptance of the ways of nature that Perdita is
to restore to her father. This restoration can be made only
when Perdita plays one further role, that of the Libyan princess.
For no sooner has she cast aside her disguise with 'Ile queene
it no inch further' than Camillo arranges to see her 'royally
appointed, as if The Scene you play, were mine' and Perdita
acquiesces with: 'I see the Play so lyes That I must beare a
part.' Her part, and that of Florizel also, is to enable Leontes to
forgive himself. Looking on them both, the old king feels time
unravel until he can understand and accept the excesses of his
own youth:

> Were I but twentie one,
> Your Fathers Image is so hit in you,
> (His very ayre) that I should call you Brother,
> As I did him, and speake of something wildly
> By vs perform'd before. . . .
>   . . . You haue a holy Father
> A gracefull Gentleman, against whose person
> (So sacred as it is) I haue done sinne,
> For which, the Heauens (taking angry note)
> Haue left me Issue-lesse: and your Father's bless'd
> (As he from Heauen merits it) with you,
> Worthy his goodnesse.   (V.i.126-30;170-6)

The irony of this is not only that Leontes' daughter and son-in-
law stand before him as he speaks, but that he should call
Polixenes 'graceful'. In fact Polixenes, in breaking the match
between Florizel and Perdita, has shown a lack of that imaginative vision, symbolised by the two lovers, which Leontes has
now acquired and which makes him the lovers' advocate,
sympathetic to Florizel's plea:

> Remember, since you ow'd no more to Time
> Then I do now.   (V.i.219-20)

The reunion of Leontes with Perdita concludes this aspect of
the play as a defence and justification of play itself. Because
Shakespeare is here concerned with recreation as re-creation,
much of the play itself seems trifling, a kind of vaudeville: the
comic turns of Autolycus, the dances, the Clown's part, the

ballads. We must not look closely for wisdom in this fooling; its purpose is to remind Everyman—Leontes and the audience— of his need for folly.

4

Besides this theme of spiritual renewal through the double operation of Grace and Nature, other meanings of the two words are at work in *The Winter's Tale*. It shares with Shakespeare's other late romances a dramatic contrast between Nature and the Graces of Art.[1] Moreover, the theme of spiritual renewal is closely paralleled by one of social reinvigoration. The question of True Nobility, which Shakespeare had already raised in *All's Well* is made a concern of *The Winter's Tale* by Shakespeare's play on several words with restrictive social meanings, of which *grace* is one. Leontes carries the title of the King's Grace (*N.E.D.*II 9), but he is none the more gracious, in the sense of being comely or blessed, on that account. Autolycus, a sometime hanger-on of the court, pretends to be outraged because the Shepherd should 'offer to haue his Daughter come into *grace*', but we have already been told that she has 'growne in *grace*' and have taken it to mean her natural dignity of bearing as well as her goodness and beauty. Again, in the use of the word *breeding* there is interplay between the widest meaning of 'begetting', the more limited social meaning of 'a good upbringing' and the most restricted meaning of 'good manners'. Polixenes, slighted by Leontes, is left 'to consider what is *breeding*, That changes thus his Manners', and in Florizel's 'She's as forward, of her *Breeding*, as She is i'th' reare' our *Birth*' there is an additional wordplay on *birth*: Perdita's only inferiority is in fact in her age, for she has not only royal birth, but also the natural good breeding of the old shepherd whose head is nothing turned when he finds himself in high society: 'we must be *gentle*, now we are Gentlemen'. The glories of our *blood* and *state* are vanity, because the vaunted blue blood turns out to be the ordinary red stuff in everyone's veins, and however stately our dignity, every man must belong to one or other of the estates which make up the state of society;

[1] See below, pp. 187-8

and Shakespeare makes subtle use of all these meanings in the course of the play.[1] Lastly, there is his use of *free* to mean 'of gentle birth' or 'of noble or honorable character' or 'at liberty'. Hermione in prison remains in her innocence as *free* as the child of whom she is delivered; to Paulina's suggestion that she take the new-born child to the king, Emilia replies:

> Most worthy Madam,
> your honor, and your goodnesse is so euident,
> That your *free* vndertaking cannot misse,
> A thriuing *yssue,* (II.ii.42-5)

and Paulina protests to the Court that the Queen is

> A gracious innocent soule,
> More free, then he is iealous. (II.iii.29-30)

In these two scenes which close the second act, the point is driven home that the truest courtesy is not a veneer of the court. Leontes' court is a beargarden and the scenes enacted there are farce on the brink of tragedy.[2] Hermione in contrast keeps court in prison with all the ceremony of innocence and so associates herself, before the trial scene, with the gracious ceremonial of Apollo's devotees, as Dion describes them:

> I shall report,
> For most it caught me, the Celestiall Habits,
> (Me thinkes I so should terme them) and the reuerence
> Of the graue Wearers. O, the Sacrifice,
> How ceremonious, solemne, and vn-earthly
> It was i'th'Offring? (III.i.3-8)

At the end of the play, the ceremony which should surround the King's Grace is restored to Leontes; his visit to Paulina is spoken of by her as a surplus of his Grace.

Before this renewal can be achieved, however, the royal grace must replenish itself from the life of nature. When the old shepherd chides Perdita for her tardiness in welcoming his

---

[1] See especially IV.iii.148; *ibid.*, 413; 439; 442.

[2] The complexity of Paulina accords with this. She is both magnificent and ludicrous. She has moreover a third aspect, that of guardian angel to Hermione and Leontes. She is very like Julia in *The Cocktail Party*—a play which is also about redemption, the eye of God and the need for ordinary mortals not to take themselves too seriously.

guests, and compares her reserve with his old wife's joviality, Shakespeare seems at first hearing to be restating the Elizabethan certainty that blood will tell; Florizel and Perdita are merely pretended shepherd and shepherdess, two figures by Fragonard superimposed on a scene by Breughel. Yet if Perdita is full of grace in every meaning of the word she owes that upbringing to the two old peasants. Polixenes' praise of the custom of grafting 'a gentler Sien, to the wildest stocke' is vivid dramatic irony, not only because he is shortly going to repudiate his theory when his son seeks to marry a shepherdess, but because Perdita's upbringing has been just such a fruitful grafting. The child of a father who has cut himself off from a wholesome rural way of living and thinking is returned by Apollo to the education of Nature, in order that ultimately court and cottage may flourish together under the sun of his favour who 'Lookes on alike'.

VIII

A WORLD OF WORDS

The plays that have been considered here in some detail are for the most part rich in wordplay. But they are equalled or surpassed in the number of their puns by other plays in the Shakespearean canon: *Love's Labour's Lost* with over two hundred; the Henry IV plays with about a hundred and fifty apiece; *Much Ado* and *All's Well* with more than a hundred each. The average number of puns in a play by Shakespeare is seventy-eight. From a record of these three thousand odd instances of wordplay in the plays and poems we might expect to emerge some pattern of a development in the use of this poetic device similar to that which has been traced in his use of imagery; or of the distribution of puns to certain types of character, or certain moments in a play's development. Unfortunately there can be no secure and objective evidence from which inductions about the development and distribution of Shakespeare's puns can be made. Every attempt to count the number of puns in a particular play yields a slightly different total, because, by the very nature of drama, every reading (and even more every performance) is a re-creation, a fresh attempt to interpret Shakespeare's intention. Nor is it easy to fix the frontiers of wordplay. Dogberry's malapropisms are not strictly wordplay and they have not been counted as such here, but they contribute as much as Beatrice's puns to the verbal gaiety of *Much Ado*. Furthermore, any attempt to tot up the puns in a particular play yields as little information as similar attempts to count recurrent images, and for the same reason, that such an assessment is quantitative and not qualitative. It overlooks the difference between the pun which is a mere squib and the one that goes off like high explosive.

Similar difficulties arise when, our instances of wordplay

duly card-indexed and counted, we try to classify them. There is no way of showing which type of Shakespearean character puns most, because Shakespeare has no types. Characters exist as part of a total situation in a particular play, and that situation may call for a punning villain in one play and for a humourless villain in another. Again, an attempt to show the distribution of puns over the course of a play has to make use of act-divisions which often seem quite arbitrary and may have nothing to do with Shakespeare's intentions. When we seek to trace the development of wordplay between the earlier and later plays, we come up against the difficulty that the order of Shakespeare's plays is not, and probably never will be, decided beyond question; and any attempt to determine which kind of pun develops at the expense of others is weakened when we realise how many quibbles belong to more than one category. The classification made in Chapter One into puns that are involuntary on Shakespeare's part, puns which are (intentionally or unintentionally) the characters', and those in which the meanings are ironically divided between Shakespeare and the character, leaves us with a good number of borderline instances. In Macbeth's words after the murder has been discovered—

> Had I but dy'd an houre before this chance,
> I had liu'd a blessed time: for from this instant,
> There's nothing serious in Mortalitie:
> All is but Toyes: Renowne and Grace is dead,
> The Wine of Life is drawne, and the meere Lees
> Is left this Vault, to brag of   (II.iii.98-103)

—it is impossible to say if the ambiguity of *blessed, mortality, grace* (and perhaps *vault* as well) belongs to Macbeth himself or only to Shakespeare. When, earlier in the same play, news comes to Macbeth that he is now thane of Cawdor and Banquo remarks to the other lords: 'Looke how our Partner's rapt' (I.iii.142), the secondary meaning of 'wrapped' is shown to be in the air by his next words:

> New Honors come vpon him
> Like our strange Garments, cleaue not to their mould,
> But with the aid of vse.

Is this the product of quite unconscious verbal linkage or is it a deliberate reinforcement of the clothing motif that runs through the play? And in *King Lear*, IV.ii.62, are we to take the ambiguity of Albany's words to Goneril—'Thou changed and *selfe couer'd* thing' to mean that Shakespeare knows Goneril to be revealing her real bad self while Albany thinks she is concealing her real good self, or that both meanings are Albany's, and mark a sudden insight into the heart of evil such as is afforded to other characters in the play?

These shifting data would be an uneasy foundation for any theories about Shakespeare's wordplay, so it is perhaps more a relief than a disappointment to find that they show too little order to render such theories tenable. It is possible to make only a few very large generalisations about the distribution and development of puns in Shakespeare. In their distribution over individual plays, we find that in twenty-three out of thirty-seven plays more than half the total instances of wordplay occur in the first two acts. An important function of wordplay is to present, by means of a word's different meanings, the conflicting issues before the audience, and once these are clear in our minds there is no further call for this type of pun. But when the occasion demands Shakespeare can quibble generously in the last acts of a play. In the last act of *Love's Labour's Lost* and that of *A Midsummer Night's Dream*, Shakespeare distinguishes the clowns from the courtiers by one group's linguistic abuses and the punning virtuosity of the other. In the fourth acts of *King Lear* and *Timon of Athens* a sharp increase in the wordplay helps to give expression to the chief character's anguish of tragic discovery.

Tragic heroes like Timon stand high in the list of Shakespeare's most punning characters; a list headed, as one might expect, by Hamlet, who quibbles some ninety times in the course of the play. Hamlet combines in his character the role of detached observer of mankind with that of a man who is horror-struck to find himself involved in deep moral corruption; and in Shakespeare these are the two types of character, represented on the one hand by Menenius and Enobarbus, on the other by Lear, whose power to see the underlying connections of things finds expression in continual wordplay. Other tragic characters

are corrupted into wordplay. Macbeth is a sufficiently apt pupil
of his wife to surpass her in the number of his puns by the end of
the play, but Iago, though he sometimes bedevils Othello into
equivocations very like his own, keeps the lead of him and all
other characters. In this he is typical of Shakespeare's villains.
Aaron speaks most of the wordplay in *Titus Andronicus*, and
Richard III puns more than any other character in *Henry VI*
part 3 and *Richard III*, though his villainies in the latter play
evoke a wild wit of resentment from Queen Elizabeth. Shylock
and Claudius stand second in the list of punning characters in
the plays in which they appear, though each speaks only a small
percentage of the total puns; and if the bawdy, unsinister wordplay of Cloten and the few, weak puns of Don John in *Much
Ado*, Proteus in *Two Gentlemen of Verona* and Antonio in
The Tempest mark out all these characters as the ineffectual
villains of tragi-comedy, what are we to make of Edmund's
failure to play with meanings? Once again, any but the broadest
generalisation proves to be unsound.

The wit of Shakespeare's characters is quickened even more
by love than it is by hate. Among Shakespeare's lovers, the
women are readier than the men with wordplay. This holds
true even of the tragic heroines, Juliet and Cleopatra. The
more romantic among the heroines of comedy—Portia, Viola,
Rosalind—outpun their lovers in their respective plays. It is
satisfying to find that the tamed shrew Katherine gets the last
word by producing one more pun than Petruchio; I make the
score sixteen-fifteen in her favour. Beatrice has an easy victory
over Benedick in the punning matches of *Much Ado*, and the
Princess in *Love's Labour's Lost* can find three puns while the
King is hunting for one; but she in her turn is far outpunned by
Berowne. In the absence of their lovers, Shakespeare's heroines
sharpen their wits on the Fool, who can usually give them as
good as they send. As we might expect, the licensed Fools, the
'naturals', and the comic servants such as the Dromios who
descend from classical comedy, all have a generous share of the
puns in the comedies. Feste utters a quarter of those that occur
in *Twelfth Night*, and Touchstone an equal proportion of the
wordplay in *As you Like It*, while the Clown is the most punning

character in *All's Well*. But in or out of the sombre household of
Shylock, Launcelot Gobbo never quibbles enough to come to
life as a comic character. For one quality is shared by all
Shakespeare's punning characters, whether heroes, villains,
lovers, *raisonneurs*, clowns, jesters: a vitality, a supercharged
mental energy, that makes them pack as much meaning into a
word as it can be made to carry. After Hamlet, no one has a
greater share of this vitality than Falstaff, who speaks about a
third of the puns in each of the plays in which he figures. The
two parts of *Henry IV* have about the same number of puns, but
the difference in quality between them helps accounts for the
difference of total effect between the two plays. Most of the
puns in part 1 are intentional and in character, the expression
of the overflowing high spirits of Falstaff, Hal and Hotspur;
but in the second part the gaiety begins to flag and Shakespeare
seeks to revive it artificially by those comic-ironic puns, which
depend on the audience seizing a meaning not grasped by the
character—usually an embarrassing kind of wit—while the
remainder of the wordplay takes the form of bitter political
innuendoes spoken by the old King and Prince John.

If punning is a sign of vitality in Shakespeare's characters,
the same thing does not necessarily hold good of Shakespeare
himself. Some of his finest plays are poor in puns—*Julius
Cæsar* has only a score, and many of these are spoken by the
irrepressible Cobbler in the opening scene. It is interesting
to notice that three other plays with very sparse wordplay—
Pericles, the third part of *Henry VI*, and *Henry VIII*—are
among those considered by many critics to be only partly by
Shakespeare. On the other hand, *A Midsummer Night's Dream*,
which is indisputably Shakespeare's, has less than thirty quibbles
—and this in spite of the fact that it is generally dated 1595-6
and so follows close upon the richly punning *Love's Labour's Lost*,
Romeo and Juliet and *Richard II*. The number of puns in a play
bears no relationship to its quality or to the type of drama to
which it belongs; no rhetorical principle of 'decorum' holds
Shakespeare back or thrusts him towards his fatal Cleopatra.
In a survey of the whole run of Shakespearean plays, I have
been able to discover only one development in his method of

playing with words. All the puns in the early plays are in character; but about the time *Richard II* is written other types of pun begin to appear, especially the kind in which the secondary meaning gives emphasis to a dominant idea of the play as a whole. The proportion of these puns remains small, but about the turn of the century an increasing number of plays show over fifteen per cent of 'non-character' puns, and in *Macbeth* the percentage is as high as fifty-three.

Other dramatists—Racine and Ibsen in particular—abide our question about their development. Shakespeare is free to turn aside from every path which the tidy academic mind would like him to tread. Yet while there is little development in Shakespeare's use of wordplay, the sequence of his plays reveals a development in his thought which is very closely associated with the use to which he puts the varied meanings of words. No one could play so long and brilliantly with words as Shakespeare did without asking himself: what is the relationship of words to things—the meaning of meaning? Nor was he the only Elizabethan to pose the question 'What's in a name?' to which one answer was provided by the great linguistic revolution of the seventeenth century. It is the nature of drama to raise questions rather than to answer them. So much of Shakespeare's dramatic writing is, however, concerned with the truth and power of words, that I think it is possible to trace his changing views of language through the sequence of his plays to something very like a conclusive answer to the problem, in as far as it affected him as a poet, in his final comedies.

1

The Elizabethan attitude towards language is assumed rather than stated, and is therefore much easier to feel than to define. Like Plato, the Elizabethans believed in the truth of names, but whereas, according to Socrates in the *Cratylus*, these right names had been given by 'the legislators', to sixteenth-century ways of thinking the right names of things had been given by God and found out by Adam. In a play on the Creation acted at Florence early in the seventeenth century, Adam takes a very long time to name the property trees, stars, and the like. It is tedious for the modern reader, but clearly it was exciting for the contemporary spectators when they heard Adam guess all the names right. Even after the seventeenth century as a whole had decided that names were arbitrary and conventional, the Cabbalists went on hunting for the natural language of Adam; and this notion of a natural language was alive and meaningful for Coleridge, who enjoyed the anti-materialist, anti-rationalist undercurrents of late seventeenth-century thought. Names, then, seemed true to most people in the sixteenth century because they thought of them as at most the images of things and at least the shadows of things, and where there was a shadow there must be a body to cast it. This view of language has died hard. The argument of sixteenth-century astronomers that no new star could be discovered because there would be no name to call it by, seems less fantastically remote from our ways of thinking when we recall that, in the present century, there were doctors who refused to accept Freud's clinical proof that men could have hysteria on the grounds that the word was derived from ὑστέρα and could therefore only apply to women. The Elizabethan faith in the rightness of words is perhaps best seen in the way their preachers handle their texts. A simple piece of poetic parallelism is developed into two topics on the assumption that where there are two words there are two things. If a word has several meanings they are shown, through the serious punning which so exasperated a later generation, to bear a kind of transcendental relationship to one another. Name puns were serious for the Elizabethans on the same principle. The bearer of a name was everything the name implied; a notion not unknown among modern parents.

Given this belief in the truth of names, a belief in the power of words through sympathetic magic followed. Where there was a name there was a thing; therefore names could conjure up things. There was, moreover, religious sanction for this traditional belief in the efficacy of words. The verbal authority given to the apostles by the Incarnate Word lived on in the Church's power to bind or loose. 'For curs wol slee—right as assoillyng savith' says Chaucer, and I think we are wrong to read our modern verbal scepticism into his words. The Word of Scripture retained the same magical power; *in principio* was, significantly, the beginning of exorcisms, and we still hold an oath on the Bible to be the most binding. Magic relied on the direct efficacy of words for spells, curses and incantations, and the superstition of dead-naming is a powerful theme of some sagas and ballads. Verbal authority passed to the king at his coronation, so that just as Christ had dubbed the apostles,[1] the king could create knights. In their turn, nobility and knighthood gave their holders the power to make their words good in challenge or vow. In the legal sphere too, the king's word was immediately effective, and so were the words spoken by those to whom he deputed legal authority, since an *act*, a *sentence*, a *deed*, were all forms of words that implied action. There is one further aspect of this belief in the efficacy of words. When Elizabethan rhetoricians spoke of the power and force of words, their meaning may have been as much literal as metaphorical. They may have thought of their words going home by physical and physiological means. Just as a glance from his lady's eye darted into the poet's eye and thence travelled down with dire results into his heart, so Hamlet's words could wring his mother's heart or cleave it in twain.

Alongside this dominant linguistic realism there had always been a certain linguistic scepticism. In the *Cratylus*, Socrates is said to be refuting the opinions of Hermogenes and of many others who declare names to be conventional. In Shakespeare's day, an abundance of popular proverbs, such as 'fine words fill not a firlot', voice the same doubt. Linguistic scepticism is also to be found in popular tales like the one of the false miracle at St Albans, about the man whose pretence of having regained his sight after lifelong blindness was exposed by his calling the king's cloak red. Shakespeare's version of the incident, in the second part of *Henry VI*, is based on the Chronicles, but it was also told to Sir Thomas More by his father. The Chronicles, too, record a number of prophecies which came true in word and not in fact, and these stories suggest a popular ironic distinction between the world of events and the conceptual world of words. Finally, linguistic scepticism of a learned kind had once flourished

[1] See Skeat's note on *Piers Plowman* II, 102 (C text).

among the English nominalists, and their habits of thought may never have been entirely suppressed.

The first reasoned protest against the magic of names was made in the soft and insidious voice of Francis Bacon. Bacon's technique for introducing a new idea was, by his own admission, to pour new meanings into old words, and this in itself constitutes a sceptical attitude to language. He is wary of a direct break with the traditional notion that words are the images of things, since this has the backing of Plato, but his project for the advancement of learning includes an impartial enquiry, to be made without deference to the Ancients, into the relationship of words to things. His own linguistic position is stated in the first book of *The Advancement of Learning*, when he says: 'Words are but the images of matter: and except they have life of reason and invention, to fall in love with them is all one as to fall in love with a picture.'[1] What is here implicit is finally made explicit by Hobbes: the look-say element of a word tells us nothing about the thing it stands for, but is a quite arbitrary mark or sign of our concept of that thing. By the 1640's, Hobbes was able to assume in his readers the same notion of the arbitrary and conventional nature of words: 'But seeing names ordered in speech (as is defined) are signs of our conceptions, it is manifest that they are not signs of the things themselves; for that the sound of this word *stone* should be the sign of a stone, cannot be understood in any other sense but this, that he that hears it collects that he that pronounces it thinks of a stone. And, therefore, that disputation, whether names signify the matter or form, or something compounded of both, and such like subtleties of the *metaphysics*, is kept up by erring men, and such as understand not the words they dispute about.'[2] Something like this theory of communication is suggested by Bacon's phrase about words' 'life of reason and invention'. But on the whole, Bacon, whose ideal of communication is demonstration in a laboratory, tends to speak of turning men's minds from the quirks of words to the subtleties of things as if communication could be made without words.

[1] *Philosophical Works*, ed. John M. Robertson (1905), p. 54.
[2] *English Works*, ed. Molesworth (1839), I, p. 17.

Several of Bacon's scientific followers saw what he had ignored, the relationship of words to things through concepts, and strove to carry out the Baconian object of cultivating 'a just . . . familiarity between the mind and things' by treating concepts simply as the string to connect the label-word with its object. Independent concepts had to be eliminated, if necessary by an act of parliament forbidding metaphorical speech. 'The Light of human minds', writes Hobbes in *Leviathan*, 'is Perspicuous Words, but by exact definitions first snuffed and purged from ambiguity.' Coleridge speaks of 'certain focal words . . .which heat and burn', but Hobbes's ideal of language is light without heat. 'Perspicuous' is a favourite word with the linguistic reformers. Language was to be translucent, displaying objects clearly, and not prismatic, reflecting back a whole spectrum of meanings. Something of this ideal underlies the poetic diction of the Augustans. A word like 'bird' could put up a series of different concepts in one mind, and different concepts in different minds, but a phrase like 'feathered tribe', which may seem to us an obfuscation, appealed to them as clarity itself, because it produced the same single, generalised concept of birdness in everyone's mind.

The *reductio ad absurdum* of linguistic scepticism is sometimes held to have been reached in 1668 when John Wilkins published his *Essay towards a Real Character and a Philosophical Language*, in which he invented a series of symbols to indicate the genus, species, subspecies and nature of everything in existence. Wilkins became a bishop in the same year, so everything in existence included the facts of the Apostles' Creed, which he wrote out for his readers in the Real Character; but it did not include fairies and fauns, for which no symbols are provided. Wilkins's project is certainly the butt of Swift, whose Lagodan School of Languages got rid of words altogether by inducing people to carry about instead the objects they wished to discuss. Any physical disadvantage in this method was outweighed—metaphorically, at any rate—by its being a really universal language. Wilkins, however, did not degrade language, so much as abandon language as a means of scientific communication. This he did because he understood better than

Hobbes the true nature of words. It was a fact that words related to concepts before things—that was why Wilkins invented his hieroglyphs in an effort to by-pass concepts; but it was not true that concepts were the mere connections between words and things. Words have a conceptual life of their own which has nothing to do with the existence or non-existence of the things they signify.

Words heat and burn with a connotative energy. For this reason, a rose could not smell as sweet by any other name. Were it called a grump it would smell as sweet as a rose only if the gardens of our childhood had been full of grumps and if poets had always likened their loves to red, red grumps. We respond to the invitation 'Do smell this rose' with all the associations of delight the word has gathered in our previous experience, of which reading is a major part. While the linguistic sceptics of the seventeenth century rightly showed there was no direct relationship between words and things, they abused the very nature of language in trying to rob words of their independent conceptual life. If a man stops when bidden to do so in the Prince's name, he does so not because the word has conjured him to a standstill, but because he has previously encountered the Prince's name in contexts which have ensured for it a response of respect and awe. Of course, if the connotations of the word have changed, it is probable that 'a will not stand'. In Shakespeare's lifetime the old hierarchy of delegated verbal authority was breaking up, and many words which had once seemed to hold magical efficacy were losing their connotative power. In the phrase of Richard of Bordeaux, men set the word against the word: the immediately realisable word of chivalry or the excommunicative power of the Pope against the decrees of absolute monarchy, the new Protestant reliance upon the word of Scripture against the traditional authority of the Church. The second Murderer of Clarence sets the word of the King's warrant against the word of the commandment to do no murder; and in the most exciting scene of *King John*, Philip's agreement with John is undermined by his previous word of promise to Constance, by her potentially effective curses, and by the papal legate's threat of excommunication. It is typical of Shakespeare's own linguistic scepticism in the early History plays that in each case the conflict is settled by expediency—that daily break-vow, Commodity. Neither the Murderer's fealty nor his faith weighs anything against the word *reward*—which has a more immediate and tangible referent than either the King's warrant or the tables of the law.

At the time he wrote these two plays, Shakespeare's experience with words had shown him that the existence of a name did not necessitate the existence of the thing named. And because the Elizabethan belief in the power of words was dependent on a belief in their truth, Shakespeare remains for a time profoundly sceptical of that power. But from his own practice as a poet comes an understanding of the conceptual power of words which has nothing to do with their rightness as names. In the great tragedies, disbelief in the truth of words is balanced by a recognition of their connotative power: and in the last plays, Shakespeare's own insight as a poet into that connotative power restores him to faith in the rightness of words. The conceptual world of words built by poetry has its own validity and truth.

2

Love's Labour's Lost is the first play in which Shakespeare boldly questions the truth of words. A repeated quibble upon *light* points to the play's central theme that words, for all their witty sparkle, are without weight or substance. In the King's opening speech, reputation, an enduring name, is the reward offered to those who will remain with him in Navarre's academy, 'Still and contemplatiue in liuing Art'. 'Living art' is an ominous phrase. It suggests *tableaux vivants*, a substitute for that experience which alone could teach the *ars vivendi*. To the will o' the wisp intellectual pretensions of the King and his companions, Berowne opposes the light of nature. The learning of the Academy is the kind that darkens counsel by words without knowledge—'Light seeking light, doth light of light beguile'. It may enable its scholars to become 'earthly Godfathers of heauens lights', but it will not give them any real knowledge of the stars they name. He is no less sceptical of the oaths imposed upon the academicians; and before long the Princess and her ladies have proved Berowne's mistrust of words to be justified. The facts of nature prove stronger than verbal resolves, and the courtiers are forced to explain away their *perjury* (a keyword of the play) with 'Vowes are but breath, and breath a vapour is'. The words and antics of the Humour characters are brought into line with this theme. Holofernes and Armado both draw out the thread of their verbosity finer than the staple of their argument. Moth's 'how easie it is to put yeres to the word three, and study three yeeres in two words, the dancing horse will tell you' parodies the attempt of the Navarre courtiers to bring things into existence by words. In the same way Costard's quibbling efforts to stave off the charges against him parody the sophistries of Berowne when he tries to prove that he and his companions are not forsworn. The play's best source of laughter is in this sleight of tongue in the verbal sceptic Berowne, as with the cry of 'O who can giue an oth? Where is a booke?' he proceeds to prove black white, and the swarthy Rosalind beautiful.

The Princess and her companions, for all the brilliance of their wordplay, are sceptical of words from the start. To prove afresh the frailty of speech, they trick their lovers into breaking a new set of vows, those of constancy:

> Now to our periurie, to adde more terror,
> We are againe forsworne in will and error. (V.ii.471-2)

and once the tersely-worded fact of the French king's death has brought to an end their wit-contests, they have no ear even for russet yeas and honest kersey noes. Only deeds can speak now:

> Your oth I will not trust: but go with speed
> To some forlorne and naked Hermitage . . . (802-3)

and Berowne is dispatched to discover the hollowness of words by jesting in a hospital. The great feast of language vanishes to the sound of harpies' wings. There is no substance in speech.

In the plays that follow this, Shakespeare questions every kind of power attributed to language. Prophecies come true

in word alone: the promise that he shall die in Jerusalem which
Henry IV cherishes as the very hope of his salvation has only a
quibbling fulfilment. Spells do not work: Hotspur jeers at
Glendower's boast that he can call spirits from the vasty deep.
Characters curse, but the stars shine still: the gardener in
Richard II is unmoved by the Queen's malediction on his plants.
Nor is there any magic in baptismal names: Hero's does not
ensure that she will be the type of faithful love, since '*Hero*
itself can blot out *Hero's* virtue'. And all Shakespeare's kings
know the vanity of what were called *additions*:

> Thinks thou the fierie Feuer will goe out
> With Titles blowne from Adulation?
> (*Henry V*, IV.i.273-4)

Shakespeare's verbal scepticism can be very sweeping in
these comedies and histories written in the 1590's. Yet it never
comprises the whole of his thought and feeling about language.
Even in the instances I have given, scepticism was not always
justified. Berowne's praise of Rosalind makes beauty the gift
of the lover's words. However the thick-spoken Hotspur may
jeer, the eloquent Glendower *is* able to call up music from the
air. The Queen's curse in *Richard II* does not blight a single
flower, but in so far as the garden is meant to stand for England,
misfortune blights the country throughout the reign of the
usurper Bolingbroke. Finally, there is something in a name
in *Much Ado*, since Leander's Hero could not be more loyal
than Claudio's Hero is finally proved to be. The ambivalence of
Shakespeare's attitude to language at this stage in his career is
most clearly seen in *Richard II*. The play might be summed up
in Hobbes's aphorism: 'Words are wise men's counters, but
the money of fools.' But if, from this point of view, Bolingbroke
is the wise man and Richard the fool, from another, dramatically
valid viewpoint, Bolingbroke is the villain and Richard the
hero. Behind the sympathetic portrayal of the defeated and
deposed king at Pomfret, turning over the gilt counterfeits of
speech which he had once taken for true gold, we feel Shakespeare's conviction that it is better to have had and lost a faith
in words than never to have surrendered to their magic.

The Henry IV plays are also deeply concerned with the truth and power of words. Here Shakespeare's flying thoughts on language all settle round the notion of Honour, a Good Name. The extreme of verbal scepticism is reached at the end of Part One by the arch-liar Falstaff: 'what is honor? a word, what is in that word honor? what is that honour? aire.'[1] In a sense, Shakespeare means Falstaff to be right. Glorious war is strongly satirised when, after all Hotspur's rhodomontade about plucking honour from the pale-faced moon, Falstaff turns over the body of Sir William Blunt to contemplate its grinning honour. But it is worth noticing that Falstaff does to the word *honour* exactly what the inventors of Newspeak, in George Orwell's totalitarian state, did to the word *free*. Because it was mere breath to them, they set to work to rob it of its emotive force for others, by restricting its use to such material and negative contexts as 'the dog is free from lice'; until, as a result of this brainwashing, a sentence such as 'All men are born free' came to seem meaningless. But for Prince Hal, the word *honour* is full of connotative life, so that he responds to its associations with honourable deeds of his own; and the final parting of Hal from Falstaff shows that Shakespeare himself believed honour to be more than a breath. In *All's Well* he goes even further and, in the King's speech upon honour and virtue, reverts to an almost magical idea of meaning. Bertram, who too easily takes the word for the thing, as his deception by Parolles indicates, will not accept Hellena as wife because she lacks a noble name. Perversely, he regards the titular honour the King is prepared to confer on Hellena as breath, a mere word. The King's long speech at this point shows, however, that, as befits a divinely appointed monarch, he regards his power to bestow honours as an extension of the original *fiat*. The inheritors of honoured names may dishonour them, but if meaning could be lost, meaning could also be found. By recognising true virtue and honour in his bestowal of titular honours, the King keeps alive the conceptual reality of the words. In giving Hellena a title of honour, he gives her her right name:

[1] Quoted from the Quarto.

> that is honours scorne,
> Which challenges it selfe as honours borne,
> And is not like the sire: Honours thriue,
> When rather from our acts we them deriue
> Then our fore-goers: the mere words, a slaue
> Debosh'd on euerie tombe, on euerie graue:
> A lying Trophee, and as oft is dumbe,
> Where dust, and damn'd obliuion is the Tombe.
> Of honour'd bones indeed, what should be saide?
> If thou canst like this creature, as a maide,
> I can create the rest: Vertue, and shee
> Is her owne dower: Honour and wealth, from mee.
> (II.iii.140-51)

This word *honour* has a special fascination for Shakespeare at this stage of his life's work because the tension between its shallow and deeper meanings corresponds to his own dilemma between linguistic scepticism and faith in the power of words. It is particularly effective as Isabella uses it five times over to Angelo in *Measure for Measure*: 'Heauen keepe your honor.' At first this seems a piece of direct, negative irony; Angelo's honour is merely his title as judge, and does not correspond to any real quality in his character. But if honour is a mere scutcheon to Angelo in the depths of his self-discovery, it is for Isabella the concept which preserves them both. Her conventional phrase is also a prayer which is answered when the Duke, in his Providential aspect, preserves Angelo from the seduction of Isabella and from the murder of her brother. In the second scene between Isabella and Angelo, the word is set against the word—not destructively, as in *King John*, but creatively, as in the third book of *Paradise Lost*: mercy against justice, the redemptive promise against the harshness of the law. And the play's conclusion sustains this by upholding the power of the Word; more particularly, of the Sermon on the Mount.

There is here strong indication of a renewed faith in language. But meanwhile, in the series of great tragedies, scepticism prevails. The stage Shakespeare's thought about language had reached towards the turn of the century can best be seen in *Julius Cæsar*. The dramatic conflict of that play is above all a conflict of linguistic attitudes. At one extreme there is Caesar himself, a superstitious man, who believes in the magic of his own name which is 'not liable to fear', and who tries to conjure with it by always speaking of himself in the third person. At the other extreme is the sceptic Cassius:

> *Brutus* and *Cæsar*: What should be in that *Cæsar*?
> Why should that name be sounded more then yours
> Write them together: Yours, is as faire a Name:
> Sound them, it doth become the mouth as well:
> Weigh them, it is as heauy: Coniure with 'em,
> *Brutus* will start a Spirit as soone as *Cæsar*.
>
> (I.ii.141-6)

For both Cassius and Brutus, words are arbitrary symbols without properties of their own. Brutus so mistrusts the effective power of words, that he will have no oaths between the conspirators. Events at first justify the scepticism of Cassius, since Caesar's name proves no talisman to him. But there is an ominous irony in Brutus's words:

> We all stand vp against the spirit of Cæsar,
> And in the Spirit of men there is no blood.
> O that we then could come by Cæsars Spirit,
> And not dismember Cæsar!   (II.i.167-70)

Words, the breathing spirit of men, are in fact the cause of much bloodshed in the remainder of the play, since the evocative power of Caesar's name is not dismembered but lives on as 'Caesarism'. The statement that '*Brutus* will start a Spirit as soone as *Cæsar*', coming from Cassius, is probably intentional irony, for he does not believe either name to have any magical power. But it is also negative dramatic irony. Brutus can *not* start a spirit because he lacks both Caesar's faith in the magic of words and Antony's knowledge of the connotative power of words. Brutus's address to the citizens approaches the Baconian ideal of establishing a just relationship between the mind and things: it is a pithy appeal to look at the facts. Its utter failure is indicated by the man in the crowd who cries out 'Let him be Cæsar.' Antony, on the contrary, has the skill not only to play upon the connotations of the word *Caesar* but also, in the course of his oration, to strip the epithet *honourable* of all its normal connotations as it is applied to Brutus. Moreover, Caesar's word lives on in Caesar's will, and thus inflames the citizens to avenge his murder. The odd episode of Cinna the poet being lynched in error for Cinna the conspirator seems irrelevant, but in fact sums up a main theme of the play. There is everything in a name—for the ignorant and irrational. The fact that none of the characters in *Julius Cæsar*, with the exception of Brutus, is morally 'placed' suggests that, while Shakespeare has cleared his thinking on language to the point where he knows words have no inherent magic but have immense connotative powers, the moral implications of this discovery, already suggested in *Richard II*, have yet to be explored. That exploration follows in the major tragedies, where the discovery that words are arbitrary signs and not right names is made by the heroes and the knowledge that the life of words is in their connotations is put to use by the villains.

3

For all Shakespeare's tragic heroes, words lose their meaning. The verbal rules and principles, the moral code by which they have lived, have ceased to correspond to things-as-they-are. The mood is that of Edmund Blunden's 'Report on Experience':

> I have been young, and now am not too old;
> And I have seen the righteous forsaken,
> His health, his honour and his quality taken.
> This is not what we were formerly told.

Given the Elizabethan belief in the rightness of words, the authoritative words of Scripture and of the moral philosophers constituted a map of experience. But for Shakespeare's tragic heroes, the map no longer corresponds to the terrain. Where a fat land was indicated there are found to be quagmires and monsters.[1] *Timon of Athens* depicts this experience with heavy moral satire, in its story of how Timon is awakened from a verbal dream in which his protestations of generosity make him rich and his guests' protestations of gratitude make them

---

[1] For a discussion of the tragic hero's 'journey without maps' see F. G. Butler: *An Aspect of Tragedy* (Grahamstown, 1953).

grateful. At the end of *Troilus and Cressida* two kinds of good name—the Virtue of Cressida, the Honour of Achilles—are found to be meaningless: 'Words, words, meere words, no matter from the heart.' The play ends where *Hamlet* begins, with the hero sustaining a shock that takes the matter out of words; at the Ghost's revelation, Hamlet wipes from his memory all 'saws of books', the commonplaces of moral philosophy. They are now 'words, words, words'—the kind of platitude spoken by Polonius, the occasional excellent moral advice of Claudius, without any relationship to the actual world of evil that has opened into Hamlet's experience.

In these three plays the discovery of facts shatter the heroes' faith in words. In other tragedies, villainy needs only words for this work. Iago himself knows words to be arbitrary signs without inherent meaning, but he makes use of the associative strength words hold for anyone as verbally credulous as Othello. A good name, reputation, is to Iago 'a most false imposition', but he plays fiendishly on Othello's belief that a good name is the immediate jewel of the soul. Othello's trust in the power of words shows itself in the white magic of an eloquence that can quell a brawl or enchant a Desdemona. This eloquence would be the sign of his nobility to the average Elizabethan, but to Shakespeare, who is a more than average Elizabethan, it is also a sign of his weakness. His insistence on his parts, his titles and his perfect soul suggests that he is bolstering up some fundamental uncertainty—about Desdemona's love, or about his place in this alien society—with the reassurance of his own rhetoric. Iago recognises this weakness. 'I neuer yet did heare: That the bruized heart was pierc'd through the eares' says Brabantio, a little before we see just this happen. Othello protests 'It is not words that moues me thus', when in fact it is nothing else. By the verbal black magic which Granville Barker neatly calls 'poetic practice bedevilled', Iago makes use of ambiguities to insert a wedge between the word and the fact for Othello. His use of *think* racks Othello between its uncertain meaning (as in 'I think it's nearly four') and its meaning of certainty based on knowledge ('I think she's a fool'). So with *seems*: 'men should be what they seem' may use *seems* as we do when we say 'it seems she is going away' or as in 'he seems better than he is'. The result of this on Othello is that words fail him in every meaning of the phrase. His splendidly assured rhetoric, in which each word was backed by fact or by the power to make it fact, breaks down into gibberish, and then is built up by Iago into a high-sounding façade of speech behind which Othello himself is in ruins.

In *King Lear*, different attitudes to the problem of language are distinguished in the wordplay upon *nothing*. When Cordelia uses the word to reply to the question 'What can you say, to draw A third, more opilent then your Sisters?' she implies that only good actions could, to her way of thinking, gain such results, and a good word is not a spell to produce a good action —it is, in fact, no *thing*. The soft words of Goneril and Regan correspond to no thing in subsequent events, but they draw a delegated power in this first scene from the associations they hold for Lear. Subsequently, Lear, like the other tragic heroes, discovers that words are no things. He has dressed himself in flattery, only to find, like Richard of Bordeaux, that the additions of a king are mere lendings. The disillusionment is so complete that at first Lear's identity seems to be lost with his titles: 'Who is it that can tell me who I am?' The Fool supplies the answer: 'now thou art an O without a figure, I am better then thou art now, I am a Foole, thou art nothing.' It is not just the voice of the child-like Fool telling the emperor he has no clothes on. It is Lear's shadow, his own insight, speaking out of his disillusionment in words; there is no reality to correspond to signs, and he himself is only a cipher.

The good, then, are wrong about words for they have, in Bacon's phrase, fallen in love with a picture; and the bad are right about them, for they know they relate to concepts, not things, and they turn this knowledge to their own advantage. Can we distinguish in the tragedies any other linguistic attitude which might lead Shakespeare out of this impasse? I think that in each major tragedy there is the hint of a reconciliation between the world of words and the world of facts—with the exception of *Macbeth* where the villain-hero ends by finding life a meaningless tale. In *King Lear*, Cordelia tries to preserve the bond of nature by giving all her words the validity of her actions. In consequence of this, she is able to bring Lear back from the despair in which he was an O without a figure, and man a poor bare forked animal, to that sober approximation of words with facts in which he sees himself as a foolish, fond old man. Othello, too, is restored to some belated faith in words by the discovery that Desdemona was true to her vows. Iago's abuse of words is finished—'From this time forth I neuer will speake word'—but with 'Soft you; a word or two before you go', Othello holds his hearers spellbound until his purpose is accomplished, and so revives for us the nobly eloquent Othello of the first two acts. *Hamlet* offers, as I have tried to show, yet another reconciliation of the world of words and that of facts, when Hamlet finds that his conviction that the world of common speech and intercourse is a make-believe world does not free him from the necessity to play his part on this great stage. Just as the Murder of Gonzago caught the conscience of the king, so Hamlet's performance of the conventional role of the Avenger may have its effect upon the world of evil revealed to him in his mother's conduct and the Ghost's disclosures.

When the seeming truth of things is found to be fiction, fiction may be the only way to the truth. Hamlet's use of the players points to a discovery Shakespeare was making about his own art. The consolation of a Shakespearean tragedy is ultimately to be found, not in any explicit statement that all is best, nor yet in the events of the play, but in the existence of the play itself. The inadequacy of words to express things has been explored and expressed in words. The poet has not only that power over words, abused by Shakespeare's villains, of playing upon the associations they hold for other people. He has also power to restore the truth of words, to ensure that where there is a word there is a thing; for in the theatre, the conceptual life of words is brought by the actors as near as it may be to actuality, so that it becomes for the audience a valid part of their experience. The golden world of Navarre is none the less real to our experience because it is shattered by the brazen fact of Mercade's message. In crying against the truth of words, Shakespeare was crying out against his own succession as a poet; and a full realisation of this seems to come in his last comedies.

4

In *The Winter's Tale* and *The Tempest*, Shakespeare's battling thoughts on language come in for the last round. The conflict of the earlier plays, between linguistic faith and linguistic scepticism, had widened, in the tragedies, into an opposition between those who have had, but lost, faith in commonplaces, the axioms of philosophy, and those who on the other hand live by no verbal principles but can always cite Scripture for their ill purposes. The final conflict is between Shakespeare's self-doubts and his faith in his own achievement; between mistrust of poetry as a mere world of words and the vindication of poetry as the only creative mode of language.

With his greatest achievement behind him, it was natural for Shakespeare in his retirement to ask himself if it had been worth doing and if it would endure, or if the best in this kind were but shadows, less valuable and less durable than the actions of life itself. As the problem of *mimesis* this had been fought out by the Ancients, and by the critics of the Renaissance in their own variations upon the *Poetics*. The debate between Perdita and Polixenes in Act IV of *The Winter's Tale* can be matched, in its use of the grafting image, by quotation from the Italian Danielli, the Frenchman Peletier and English Puttenham.[1] Perdita will have no streaked gilly-flowers:

> For I haue heard it said,
> There is an Art, which in their pidenesse shares
> With great creating-Nature.
> *Pol.* Say there be:
> Yet Nature is made better by no meane,
> But Nature makes that Meane: so ouer that Art,
> (Which you say addes to Nature) is an Art
> That Nature makes.   (IV.iv.86-92)

The meaning of this last phrase is uncertain; it could mean that Nature makes Art, but it can also mean that Art makes Nature

---

[1] See Harold J. Wilson: 'Nature and Art in *The Winter's Tale* IV.iv.86 following', *Shakespeare Association Bulletin* 1943.

because, in Sir Thomas Browne's phrase, Nature is the Art of God. The same problem of the inferiority or superiority of art to nature teases Keats out of thought when he looks at the Grecian Urn, too cold and motionless to satisfy as a perpetuation of the life it depicts. Is the lifeless permanence of art better than the transience of 'all breathing human passion'? Hokusai can still a breaking wave for the pleasure of many centuries, but his wave does not still move. But here Shakespeare has the advantage over the painter and even over the craftsman whose Chinese jar, in T. S. Eliot's phrase 'Still moves perpetually in its stillness'. As soon as he has shown that the relationship of art to nature cannot be solved by the hen-and-egg argument of Perdita and Polixenes, he gives us one resolution of the problem in Perdita's dance and in Florizel's description of her dancing:

> When you do dance, I wish you
> A waue o'th Sea, that you might euer do
> Nothing but that: moue *still*, *still* so:
> And owne no other Function.   (140-3)

Drama comes nearest to life of all forms of *mimesis* because it is continually reanimated by living actors; and in acknowledgement of this Shakespeare entrusts the weight of the play's meaning at this climax to a boy-actor's silent mimetic art. When Perdita dances, the old antagonism of art and nature disappears, for there is no way in which we can tell the dancer from the dance.

This is Shakespeare's first statement in *The Winter's Tale* of the interdependence of art and nature, and his first claim for drama's power to reconcile them as it is represented in Perdita's make-believe of Queen of the Feast. The whole scene of the sheep-shearing feast is one of the finest celebrations in English Renaissance literature of the plenitude and renewing vigour of 'great creating Nature'. It is matched only by Spenser's myth of the Garden of Adonis in Book III of *The Faerie Queene*. In one way the resemblance of the two passages is very close. In each the poet seems to be seeking, but failing to find, the satisfaction of a personal desire. The exiled Spenser craves a stability which is not to be found even in 'the first seminary of all things':

For all that liues, is subject to that law:
All things decay in time, and to their end do draw.

Time is the troubler of Spenser's garden, just as Time, in the
person of the wintry Polixenes, tramples Perdita's flowers.
Perdita is a nature spirit, the symbol of the renewing seasons,
welcome to her father even before her recognition 'As is the
Spring to th'Earth'. But because Nature is at the mercy of Time,
Leontes' renewal through Perdita's return is only a token
rejuvenation; the life of the next generation is their own, not
ours.

The past, however, is restored to Leontes in the person of
Hermione, whose revival is Shakespeare's second statement of
drama's power to reconcile art and nature. I have suggested
earlier that Perdita represents natural goodness. In this aspect
of Nature she helps in the regeneration of Everyman Leontes
but she cannot accomplish it alone; the priestess-like Paulina
must invoke for him the Grace of Heaven as it is represented
in the rejected but faithful Hermione. Hermione represents also
the graces of art which must be added to the delights of nature
before Leontes is restored to a full and good life. When Hermione plays at being a statue that comes to life, Shakespeare is
not just trifling with a piece of stage-business borrowed from
the masque. The scene is Shakespeare's affirmation of his faith
as a dramatist that the best in this kind are much more than
shadows. Art, represented by the play-acting Hermione, replaces the destroyed illusion of Leontes by 'a new truth' bringing with it

> a new peace, having heard the solemn
> Music strike and seen the statue move
> To forgive our illusion.[1]

Auden's words recall *A Winter's Tale*, but they define the
ultimate mood of *The Tempest*, in which Shakespeare once again
questions and vindicates the value of the poet's work. The
contention in *The Winter's Tale* is between Art and Nature; in
The Tempest, it is rather between Art and Action. A self-doubt
as dark as that of the later Ibsen makes itself felt at several

---

[1] W. H. Auden, *The Sea and the Mirror*, p. 25 (in *For the Time Being*, 1945).

points in the play. Prospero is haunted by the recollection of how he lost his dukedom by neglecting worldly business for the bookish world of words. Within the play, he nearly loses his life when, absorbed in the presentation of his masque for the lovers, he forgets the plot of Caliban and his confederates; but with the intrusion of reality into Prospero's beating mind the whole spectacle of plenty, harmony and fertility vanishes into thin air.

Yet the truth of poetry, the validity of the conceptual life in words, is reasserted after a struggle against thoughts such as these. Prospero's neglect of life for art is more than atoned for in his use of his magician's art to set all to rights in the courts of Naples and Milan. Caliban's warning to the conspirators:

> Remember
> First to possesse his Bookes; for without them
> Hee's but a Sot, as I am, (III.ii.102-4)

is, by its truth and untruth, the play's first vindication of art. The second comes when Prospero himself likens the vanished masque to the fading pageant of nature; for we feel that, in some Aristotelian sense of *mimesis*, the shadow of a shadow may well be nearer to a substantial reality than is the fading vicissitude it imitates. The final and the strongest vindication of Prospero's art is spoken at the end of the play by Gonzalo:

> In one voyage
> Did Claribell her husband finde at Tunis,
> And Ferdinand her brother, found a wife,
> Where he himselfe was lost: Prospero, his Dukedome
> In a poor Isle: and all of vs, our selues,
> When no man was his owne. (V.i.208-13)

The world of words had once seemed to Shakespeare tragically incompatible with the world of things. Now he finds in the world built from Prospero's words of magic the truth of what we are. Belief in words is foremost among the lost things which are found again in Shakespeare's final comedies.

INDEX

Plays and Poems of Shakespeare

Words and phrases discussed or referred to in the text